KAREN BROWN'S

Irish

Country Inns & Itineraries

KAREN BROWN'S

Irish Country Inns & Itineraries

Written by

JUNE BROWN

Sketches by Barbara Tapp
Cover Painting by Jann Pollard

Travel Press
Karen Brown's Country Inn Series

Travel Press editors: Iris Sandilands, Karen Brown, Clare Brown, Susanne Lau Alloway
Technical support: William H. Brown III; Aide-de-camp: William H. Brown
Illustrations: Barbara Tapp; Cover painting: Jann Pollard
Maps: Susanne Lau Alloway—Greenleaf Design & Graphics

Distributed USA & Canada: The Globe Pequot Press, tel: (203)395-0440, fax: (203) 395-0312
Box 833, Old Saybrook, CT 06475

Distributed Europe: Springfield Books Ltd., tel: (01484) 864 955, fax: (01484) 865 443
Norman Road., Denby Dale, Huddersfield HD8 8TH, W. Yorkshire, England,
A catalog record for this book is available from the British Library

Distributed Australia: Little Hills Press Pty. Ltd., tel: (02) 437-6995, fax: (02) 438-5762
1st Floor, Regent House, 37-43 Alexander St, Crows Nest NSW 2065, Australia

Distributed New Zealand: Tandem Press Ltd., tel: (0064) 9 480-1452, fax: (0064) 9 480 1455
P.O. Box 34-272, Birkenhead, Auckland 10, New Zealand

Library of Congress Cataloging-in-Publication Data

Brown, June, 1949-
    Karen Brown's Irish country inns & itineraries / written by June
Brown ; sketches by Barbara Tapp ; cover painting by Jann Pollard
      p. cm. -- (Karen Brown's country inns series)
 Includes index.
 ISBN 0-930328-26-4 : $16.95
  1. Hotels--Ireland--Guidebooks. 2. Ireland--Guidebooks. 3. Ireland--Guidebooks.
I. Brown, Karen, 1949- . II. Title. III. Title: Irish country
inns and itineraries. IV. Series.
TX907.5.I73B76 1994
647.9441501--dc20
                       94-16475
                         CIP

For Pam and Ann

KAREN BROWN TITLES

California Country Inns & Itineraries

English Country Bed & Breakfasts

English, Welsh & Scottish Country Hotels & Itineraries

French Country Bed & Breakfasts

French Country Inns & Itineraries

German Country Inns & Itineraries

Irish Country Inns & Itineraries

Italian Country Bed & Breakfasts

Italian Country Inns & Itineraries

Spanish Country Inns & Itineraries

Swiss Country Inns & Itineraries

Contents

Foreword

Irish Country Inns & Itineraries is written specifically for those individuals who want to experience a slice of Irish life staying as guests in country houses, farms, and small, family-run hotels. Our guide is not written for those who want the symmetry of worldwide hotel chains with their identical bathrooms and minibars. The fondest memories of a visit to the Emerald Isle are those of its warm-hearted, friendly people, and there can be no better way to meet the people than to stay with them in their homes. To keep you on the right track we have formed itineraries linking the most interesting sightseeing, enabling you to spend from a few weeks to a month exploring this fascinating island. In addition, we have designed a walking tour of Dublin's fair city that blends culture, history, shopping, and Guinness. In the title the term "inn" refers to places to stay that we regularly visit, and where we enjoy staying, establishments that are our favorites, preferably owned and run by a welcoming family. These are the kinds of places where you are expected to carry your own bag; service may not be the most efficient and occasionally the owners have their eccentricities, which all adds to the allure. There are enough recommendations in every price category to enable you to tailor your trip to your budget. Rates are quoted in Irish punts in the Republic of Ireland and pounds sterling in Northern Ireland. We have recommended accommodation in the widest of price ranges, so please do not expect the same standard of luxury at, for example, Foxmount Farm, as Marfield House—there is no comparison—yet each is outstanding in what it offers. Please write to us—your comments and suggestions are invaluable.

Karen Brown's Guides
P.O. Box 70
San Mateo CA 94401
USA

An Irish Blessing

May the road rise to meet you,

May the wind be always at your back,

May the sun shine warm upon your face,

May the rains fall soft upon your fields,

And, until we meet again,

May God hold you in the palm of his hand.

Introduction

Writers wax lyrical about Ireland's spectacular scenery: ever-changing landscapes, splendid seascapes, purple moorlands, monastic ruins, enchanting lakes, towering fortresses, and vast patchworks of fields spread in every shade of green—believe every word they say. But realize that it's the people with their open friendliness and warmth of welcome that make a visit to Ireland special. This guide is all about Irish hospitality and staying in places where you are a house guest rather than a customer. Ireland is not conducive to rushing: the narrow country roads lend themselves to exploration at a leisurely pace where you return the smile and wave of greeting of those you pass. Take time to stop at a pub and be drawn into conversation, and when you get lost, ask directions and learn a bit of history or folklore, as a bonus, along with the directions, leading you to ask again farther down the road.

About Ireland

The following pointers are given in alphabetical order, not in order of importance.

CLIMATE

It has been said that there is no such thing as climate in Ireland—only weather, and no such thing as bad weather—only the wrong clothes. This is because the changes in conditions from day to day and even from hour to hour seem greater than the changes from one season to the next. The Atlantic Ocean and the air masses moving east give Ireland very little seasonal variation in temperature, producing mild winters and cool summers. The ocean's influence is strongest near the coast, especially in winter when areas bordering the sea are milder than those inland. Coastal areas, particularly in the west, also have less variation in temperature between day and night. Even when it rains, and it does, it never pours—it's just soft Irish rain that keeps the isle emerald. The best thing is to be prepared for sun and sudden squalls at all times.

CLOTHING

Ireland is an easygoing place and casual clothes are acceptable everywhere, even at the fanciest restaurants. Because the weather is changeable, layers of sweaters and shirts that can be added to and removed are recommended. A lightweight, waterproof jacket with a hood is indispensable. Do not haul huge suitcases into B&Bs: rather, we suggest that you have a small suitcase (of the size that fits under your airline seat) that you take into the places you stay, leaving most of your clothes in your large suitcase in the car.

CURRENCY

The unit of currency in the Republic of Ireland is punts, in Northern Ireland pounds sterling. The two currencies do not have equal value. Both are abbreviated to £.

DRIVING

It is to the countryside that you must go, for to visit Ireland without driving through the country areas is to miss the best she has to offer. Driving is on the left-hand side of the road which may take a little getting used to if you drive on the right at home, so avoid driving in cities until you feel comfortable with the system. If your arrival city is Dublin, do not pick your car up until you are ready to leave for the countryside. Your car will not be an automatic unless you specifically reserve one. A valid driver's license from your home country is required. Car hire is expensive, so shop around before making a reservation. If you intend to travel in Northern Ireland and rent your car in the Republic, make certain that the car company permits their car to be taken into Northern Ireland. Petrol (gasoline) is extremely expensive.

In the Republic, people by and large do not use road numbers when giving directions: they refer to roads as where they might lead to, e.g., the Cork road. To add to the confusion, new road signs quote distances in kilometers, while old signposts are in miles. The Irish seem to use neither, always quoting distances in the number of hours it takes them to drive.

The types of roads found in Ireland are as follows:

MOTORWAYS: The letter "M" precedes these fast roads which have two or three lanes of traffic either side of a central divider. Motorways are more prevalent in Northern Ireland though they are becoming more common around larger towns in the Republic.

NATIONAL ROADS: The letter "N" precedes the road number in the Republic, while in Northern Ireland the road number is preceded by the letter "A." They are the straightest and most direct routes you can take when motorways are not available.

REGIONAL ROADS: The letter "R" precedes the road number on maps, but their numbers rarely, if ever, appear on signposts. They are usually wide enough for two cars or one tractor.

Off the major routes, road signs are not posted as often as you might wish, so when you drive it's best to plan some extra time for asking the way. Asking the way does have its advantages—you get to experience Irish directions from natives always ready to assure you that you cannot miss your destination—which gives you the opportunity of asking another friendly local the way when you do. One of the joys of meandering along sparsely traveled country roads is rounding a bend to find that cows, sheep, and donkeys take precedence over cars as they saunter up the middle of the road. When you meet someone on a country road, do return their salute.

Introduction: About Ireland

INFORMATION

The Irish Tourist Board and Northern Ireland Tourist Board are invaluable sources of information. They can supply you with details on all areas of Ireland and, at your request, specific information on accommodation in homes, farmhouses, and manors as well as information on festivals, fishing, and the like. In Ireland, the Tourist Offices, known as Bord Failte, have specific information on their area and will, for a small fee, make lodging reservations for you. Their major offices are located as follows:

BELFAST

Irish Tourist Board, 53 Castle Street, Belfast BT1 1NB, tel: (01232) 327888, fax: (01232) 240201

Northern Ireland Tourist Board, 59 North Street, Belfast BT1 1NB, tel: (01232) 231221, fax: (01232) 240960

DUBLIN

Irish Tourist Board, Baggot Street Bridge, Dublin 2, tel: (01) 6765871, fax: (01) 6764764

Northern Ireland Tourist Board, 16 Nassau Street, Dublin 2, tel: (01) 6791977, fax: (01) 6791863

FRANKFURT

Irish Tourist Board, Untermainanlage 7, 6000 Frankfurt/Main, tel: (069) 236 492, fax: (069) 234 626

Northern Ireland Tourist Board, Taunusstrasse 52-60, 60329 Frankfurt/Main, tel: (069) 234 504, fax: (069) 238 0717

LONDON .

All Ireland Tourism, British Travel Centre, 4 Lower Regent Street, London SW1Y 4PQ, tel: (0171) 839 8416, fax: (0171) 839 6179

NEW YORK

Irish Tourist Board, 345 Park Ave, New York NY 10017, tel: (800) 223 6470, fax: (212) 371 9052

Northern Ireland Tourist Board, 551 Fifth Avenue, Suite 701, New York NY 10176, tel: (212) 922 0101, fax: (212) 922 0099

SYDNEY

All Ireland Tourism, 36 Carrington Street, Sydney NSW 2000, tel: (02) 299 6177, fax: (02) 299 6323

TORONTO

Irish Tourist Board, 160 Bloor Street East, Suite 934, Toronto M4W 1B9, tel: (416) 929 2777, fax: (416) 929 6783

Northern Ireland Tourist Board, 111 Avenue Road, Suite 450, Toronto M5R 3J8, tel: (416) 925 6368, fax: (416) 961 2175

Introduction: About Ireland

MAPS

Our preference is for the Michelin map of Ireland where the scale is 4 kilometers to 1 centimeter (1/400,000). Each driving itinerary is preceded by a map showing the route, and each hotel listing is referenced to a map at the back of the book. We have tried to include as much information as possible, but you will need a more detailed map to outline your travels.

PUBS

Ireland's pubs will not disappoint—if you do not expect sophisticated establishments. Most of the 12,000 pubs where the Irish share ideas over frothing pints of porter have a contagious spirit and charm. Stop at a pub and you'll soon be drawn into conversation. At local pubs musicians and dancers perform for their own enjoyment, their audience being those who stop by for a drink. If this kind of entertainment appeals to you, ask someone wherever you are staying to recommend a local pub that will have live music that night.

ROOTS

The Potato Famine of the 1840s cut population by a fourth. Through the lean decades that followed, the Irish left by the thousands to make new lives primarily in the United States, Canada, Australia, and New Zealand. The first step in tracing your Irish roots is to collect together as much information on your Irish antecedent as possible and to find out from relatives or documents (death or marriage certificates) just where he or she came from in Ireland. Armed with this information your choices are several:

DO IT YOURSELF: If your ancestors hailed from Southern Ireland, visit the genealogical offices on Kildare Street in Dublin. If your ancestors came from Northern Ireland, visit the Public Record Office of Northern Ireland, 66 Balmoral Avenue, Belfast BT9 6YN which is open for visitors to do their own research.

HAVE SOMEONE DO IT FOR YOU: The genealogical office charges a small fee, but due to a huge backlog often takes more than a year to do a general search. Write to Chief Herald, General Office of Ireland, Kildare Street, Dublin 2, enclosing what you know about your ancestors.

A reputable genealogical service such as Hibernian Researchers, 22 Windsor Road, Dublin 6 charges higher fees, moves faster, and produces a more comprehensive report. Write to them for details.

If your ancestors came from Northern Ireland, send what you know about your ancestors, along with a letter, to one of the following: Ulster Historical Foundation, 66 Balmoral Avenue, Belfast BT9 6NY; General Register Office, Oxford House, 55 Chichester Street, Belfast BT1 4HL; Presbyterian Historical Society, Church House, Fisherwick Place, Belfast BT1 6DU.

The major tourist offices have brochures on tracing your ancestors that give more detailed information and provide information on publications that may be of interest to those of Irish descent.

Introduction: About Ireland

SHOPPING

Prices of goods are fairly standard throughout Ireland, so make your purchases as you find items you like since it is doubtful that you will find them again at a less expensive price. The most popular items to buy are hand-knitted sweaters, tweeds, crystal, china, and hand-embroidered linens.

Value Added Tax (VAT) is included in the price of your purchases. There is usually a minimum purchase requirement, but it is possible for visitors from non-EEC countries to get a refund of the VAT on the goods they buy in one of two ways:

1. If the goods are shipped overseas direct from the point of purchase, the store can deduct the VAT at the time of sale.

2. Visitors taking the goods with them should ask the store to issue a VAT refund receipt. A passport is needed for identification. On departure, BEFORE you check in for your flight, go to the office at Shannon or Dublin Airport. Your receipts will be stamped and they may ask to see your purchases. You will be given a cash refund in the currency of your choice.

About Itineraries

To keep you on the right track we have formed driving itineraries covering the most interesting sightseeing. If time allows, you can link the four driving itineraries together and travel around Ireland. Each itinerary explores a region's scenic beauty, history, and culture, and avoids its large cities. At the beginning of each itinerary we suggest our recommended pacing to help you decide the amount of time to allocate to each region. Along the way we suggest alternative routes and side trips. Each itinerary map shows all of the towns and villages in which we have a recommended place to stay. The capricious changes in the weather mean that often what appears sparkling and romantic in sunshine, appears dull and depressing under gathering storm clouds. If the weather is stormy, find a nice place with good company. Once the rain clears there is much to see. Each itinerary is preceded by an artist's impression of the proposed route. We suggest that you outline this on a commercial map: our preference is for the Michelin map of Ireland where the scale is 4 kilometers to 1 centimeter (1/400,000).

Overview of Driving Itineraries

The North

Rosgull Peninsula

Tory Island

Giant's Causeway

Glencolumbkille

Donegal

Belfast

Céide Fields

Sligo

The West

Lough Gill

Crossmolina

Achill Island

Connemara

Inishbofin Island

Clifden

Galway

Dublin

Dublin Walking Tour

Burren

Aran Islands

Kilkenny

Limerick

Cashel

Dingle Peninsula

Waterford

The Southeast

Killarney

Blarney

Ring of Kerry

Kenmare

Cork

Skellig Michael

Kinsale

Beara Peninsula

The Southwest

Intinerary Route

Alternative Routes & Sidetrips

About Places To Stay

This book does not cover the many modern hotels in Ireland with their look-alike bedrooms, televisions, and direct-dial phones. Rather, it offers a selection of personally recommended lodgings that cover the widest range from a very basic, clean room in a simple farmhouse to a sumptuous suite in an elegant castle hotel. In many, the decor is less than perfect, but the one thing they all have in common is that their owners offer wholehearted hospitality. We have inspected each and every one, and have stayed in a great many. The accommodations selected are the kind of places that we enjoy. We have tried to be candid and honest in our appraisals and to convey each listing's special flavor so that you know what to expect and will not be disappointed.

To help you appreciate and understand what to expect when staying at listings in this guide, the following pointers are given in alphabetical order, not in order of importance.

CHILDREN

The majority of listings in this guide welcome children. A great many places offer family rooms with a double and one or two single beds in a room. If you want to tuck your children up in bed and enjoy a leisurely dinner, many of the listings will with notice provide an early supper for children.

CHRISTMAS

If the information section indicates that the listing is open during the Christmas holiday season, there is a very good chance that it offers a festive Christmas package.

CLASSIFICATION OF PLACES TO STAY

To help you select the type of accommodation you are looking for, we classify the last line of our descriptions as follows:

B&B: a private home, not on a farm, that offers bed and breakfast.

B&B WITH STABLES: accommodation and the opportunity to ride.

CITY HOTEL: a hotel in Dublin.

COUNTRY HOUSE: more upmarket than a farmhouse or a B&B, a home of architectural interest without all the amenities offered by a country house hotel.

COUNTRY HOUSE HOTEL: a home or establishment of architectural interest with a restaurant, bar, and staff other than the proprietors.

FAMILY HOTEL: a small, family-run hotel in a town.

FARMHOUSE B&B: a private home on a farm that offers bed and breakfast.

GUESTHOUSE: a small, usually family-run hotel corresponding roughly to a Continental pension.

INN: a pub with rooms.

LUXURY RESORT: an architecturally interesting hotel that is a destination in itself. It usually offers such facilities as gymnasium, swimming pool, golf course, riding, fishing, and shooting.

RESTAURANT WITH ROOMS: a restaurant that also offers bed and breakfast accommodation.

CREDIT CARDS

Whether an accommodation accepts payment by credit card is indicated in the accommodation description section using the terms: none, AX-American Express, EC-Eurocard, MC-Master Card and Access, VS-Visa, or simply, all major.

DIRECTIONS

We give concise driving directions to guide you to the listing which is often in a more out-of-the-way place than the town or village in the address. We would be very grateful if you would let us know of cases where our directions have proved inadequate.

ELECTRICITY

The voltage is 240. Most hotels, guesthouses, and farmhouses have American-style razor points for 110 volts. If you are coming from overseas, it is recommended that you take only dual voltage appliances and a kit of electrical plugs. Your host can usually loan you a hairdryer or an iron.

HIDDEN IRELAND

Several of the listings are members of Hidden Ireland, a consortium of private houses that open their doors to a handful of guests at a time. All houses are of architectural merit and character with owners to match. These are the kind of houses where you can indulge yourself by staying with people who have mile-long driveways, grand dining rooms watched over by redoubtable ancestors, four-poster beds which you have to climb into, and vast billiard rooms. The kind of places most of us can only dream of living, but where you are very welcome as guests because you are the ones who help the owners pay their central heating bills, school fees, and gardeners. Guests become a part of the household—you are not expected to scuttle up to your room while family life carries on around you. Everyone usually dines together round a polished table, and unless you

make special requests, you eat what is served to you. The conversation flows and you meet those you might never have met elsewhere. Early or late in the season you may find that you are the only guests in these houses and you can enjoy a romantic candlelit dinner in a house full of character and charm. There are lakes full of salmon and stylish modern bedrooms at Delphi, gigantic old-fashioned bedrooms at Temple House, homey friendliness at Lorum Old Rectory, and innumerable ancestral portraits at Tempo Manor. We have listed members of this group at the back of the book. A brochure listing all members of Hidden Ireland is available from Irish tourist offices or from Hidden Ireland, Kensington Hall, Grove Park, Dublin 6, Ireland, tel: (01) 686463, fax: (01) 686578.

IRISH COUNTRY HOUSES ASSOCIATION

Several of the listings are members of Irish Country Houses , usually referred to as The Blue Book because of the distinctive blue color of its brochure. This is an association of owner-managed country houses, hotels, and restaurants. The majority of the members are country house hotels offering accommodation in charming surroundings, restaurants, bars, and room service. However there are several members who welcome guests to their ancestral homes on house-party lines (much as members of Hidden Ireland) with no bar and a set dinner menu. We have listed members of this group at the back of the book. The Blue Book, listing all members of the association, is available from Irish tourist offices and members.

MAPS

Each place to stay is referenced to one of the maps at the back of the book. These are an artist's renderings and are not intended to replace commercial maps. Maps in this book can be cross-referenced with the Michelin map of Ireland where the scale is 4 kilometers to 1 centimeter (1/400,000).

MEALS

Owners of guesthouses, farmhouses, and bed and breakfasts are usually happy to serve an evening meal if you make arrangements before noon. Country houses offer a set menu of more elaborate fare and most offer interesting wines—arrangements to dine must be made before noon. Hotels offer menus and wine lists, giving you more dining choices. Our suggestion is that you make arrangements for dinner on the night of your arrival at the same time you make reservations for accommodation.

RATES

Rates are those quoted to us either verbally or by correspondence for the 1995 high season (June, July, and August). The rates given are for the least expensive double room (2 people) inclusive of taxes and, in most cases, breakfast. OR we quote the cost of bed and breakfast per person per night in a room that has ensuite facilities (whenever this is available). When a listing does not include breakfast in its rates we mention this in the description. We feel a great deal of resentment when an obligatory service charge of 10-15% is added to the bill and feel that establishments often use this as a way of padding their rates. Forewarned is forearmed and we have stated if an establishment charges a service charge. Please ALWAYS CHECK prices and terms when making a reservation. Rates are quoted in Irish punts or pounds sterling in Northern Ireland.

Prices vary considerably and on the whole reflect the type of house in which you will be staying. From the charm of a simple farmhouse to the special ambiance of a vast sporting estate, each listing reflects the Irish way of life.

RESERVATIONS

Reservations should always be made in advance for Dublin accommodation. In the countryside space is not so tight and a nice room can often be had simply by calling in the morning. July and August are the busiest times and if you are traveling to a popular spot such as Killarney, you should make advance reservations. Be specific as to what your needs are, such as a ground-floor room, ensuite shower, twin beds, family room. Check the prices which may well have changed from those given in the book (summer 1995). Ask what deposit to send or give your credit card number. Tell them about what time you intend to arrive and request dinner if you want it. Ask for a confirmation letter with brochure and map to be sent to you. There are several options for making reservations:

LETTER: If you write for reservations you will usually receive your confirmation and a map. You should then send your deposit.

FAX: Our preference for making a reservation. It is the quickest and most efficient way to obtain reservations.

TELEPHONE: You have your answer immediately, so if space is not available, you can then decide on an alternative. (If calling from the United States allow for the time difference [Ireland is five hours ahead of New York] so that you can call during their business day. Dial 011 [the international code], 353 [Ireland's code] OR 44 [Northern Ireland's code], then the city code [dropping the 0], and the telephone number.)

U.S. REPRESENTATIVE: We have listed the U.S. representatives along with the hotels they service at the back of the book. If you live in the United States, this is an extremely convenient way for you to secure a reservation. However, sometimes representatives charge for their services, or only reserve the more expensive rooms or quote a higher price to cover themselves against currency fluctuations. We have listed the various hotel representatives as a convenience for our readers: we are in no way affiliated with any of the hotel representatives and cannot be responsible for any bookings made through them.

SIGHTSEEING

We have tried to mention sightseeing attractions near each lodging to encourage you to spend several nights in each location.

Dublin Walking Tour

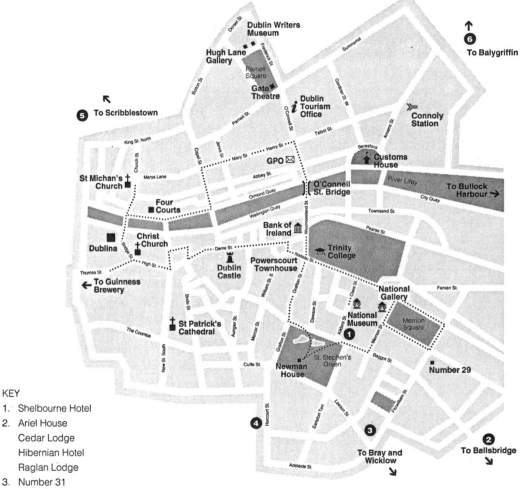

KEY
1. Shelbourne Hotel
2. Ariel House
   Cedar Lodge
   Hibernian Hotel
   Raglan Lodge
3. Number 31
4. Russell Court Hotel
5. Avondale House
6. Belcamp Hutchinson

19

Dublin Walking Tour

"In Dublin's fair city where the girls are so pretty," goes the popular old ballad. The girls are certainly pretty and the city fair if you can overlook the rash of modern office developments begun in the 1960s and the large areas that have been razed and seemingly abandoned. Dublin now appears to have seen the error of its ways and efforts are being made to restore what the bulldozers have spared. A car is more trouble than it is worth in Dublin. If your visit here is at the outset of your trip, we suggest that you not get your car until you are ready to leave or, if Dublin is a stop on your trip, park it for the duration of your stay. Dublin is a walking town, so don comfortable shoes and set out to explore the buildings, streets, and shops of this bustling, friendly city. If you feel weary along the way there is no shortage of pubs where you can revive yourself with a refreshing drink.

Dublin Walking Tour

RECOMMENDED PACING: If you select a few museums that appeal to you and simply skirt the exterior of the others, this walking tour can be accomplished in a day, which means that you will need two nights' accommodation in Dublin.

A convenient place to begin your tour is the **O'Connell Street Bridge** which spans the River Liffey, dividing the north from the south of Dublin. (It is also just by the city center terminus for buses: those displaying "An Lar," meaning city center, usually end up here.) Turn south into **Westmorland Street** past the somber, windowless **Bank of Ireland** that began life in 1729 as the seat of the Irish parliament. Cross the street and enter through the front arch of **Trinity College** into the cobbled square. Founded in 1591 by Elizabeth I, it contains a fine collection of buildings from the 18th to the 20th centuries. Cross the square to the jewel of Trinity College where a display center in the library houses the *Book of Kells*, a Latin text of the Four Gospels. A page of this magnificent illuminated manuscript is turned every month and if you are not overly impressed by the page on display, return to the library bookshop and browse through a reproduction. (Open daily.) A recent introduction at the College is **The Dublin Experience**, a sophisticated audio-visual presentation that orients you to the main events of Irish history. (Open daily Jun-Oct.)

Retrace your steps to the front gate and turn south into **Grafton Street** which is closed to vehicles and teems with people. Its large modern department store, **Switzers,** and the more traditional store, **Brown Thomas,** are popular places to shop. Johnston's Court, a narrow lane, leads you to **Powerscourt Townhouse**. This was a courtyard house built between 1771 and 1774 which has been converted into a shopping center by covering the courtyard with a glass roof and building balconies and stairways against the brick facades forming the quadrangle. The center space and balconies are given over to cafe tables and chairs—secure a balcony table and watch Dubliners at their leisure.

Rivaling Powerscourt Townhouse as a coffee or lunch rendezvous is **Bewley's Cafe**, on Grafton Street, a landmark, old-fashioned tea and coffee shop frequented by Dubliners.

Upstairs genteel waitress service is offered while downstairs it's self-service tea, coffee, sticky buns, sausages, chips, and the like. The food is not outstanding, but the atmosphere is very "Dublin."

At the end of Grafton Street dodge the hurrying buses and cross into the peaceful tranquillity of **St Stephen's Green**, an island of flowers, trees, and grass surrounding small lakes dotted with ducks. On the far side of the square at 85 and 86 St Stephen's Green is **Newman House** which was once the home of the old National University (later University College Dublin) which boasted James Joyce amongst its distinguished pupils. Number 85 is restored to its pristine, aristocratic years of the 1730s. On the ground floor are wall reliefs of the god Zeus and his nine muse daughters, done elaborately in stucco. A staircase of Cuban mahogany leads to a reception room with more riotous plasterwork figures on the ceiling. Number 86 has some rooms with interesting associations with the Whaley family and Gerald Manley Hopkins, and the Bishops Room has been restored to its Victorian splendor. (Closed Mon, tel: 01 475 7255.)

Shelbourne Hotel

Return to the northern side of the square past the landmark **Shelbourne Hotel**, a perfect place to enjoy a sedate afternoon tea of dainty sandwiches, buttered scones with whipped cream, and homemade cakes and pastries (3:00 pm to 5:30 pm). Follow **Merrion Row** and turn left into **Merrion Street** passing **Leinster House**, the Irish Houses of Parliament. It consists of two chambers—the Dáil, the lower house, and the Seanad, the upper house or senate. You can tour the building when parliament is not in session. Adjacent to the parliament building is the **National**

Gallery of Ireland which is a Victorian building with about 3,000 works of art. There's a major collection of Ireland's greatest painter, Jack Yeats, and works by Canaletto, Goya, Titian, El Greco, Poussin, Manet, Picasso, and many others. (Open daily, tel: 01 661 5133.)

Merrion Square is one of Dublin's finest remaining Georgian squares and the onetime home of several famous personages—William Butler Yeats lived at 82 and earlier at 52, Daniel O'Connell at 51, and Oscar Wilde's parents occupied number 1. The jewel of Merrion Square is **Number 29** Lower Fitzwilliam Street (corner of Lower Fitzwilliam Street and Upper Mount Street), a magnificently restored, late-18th-century townhouse. From the basement through the living rooms to the nursery and playrooms, the house is meticulously furnished in the style of the period (1790-1820)—real "Upstairs Downstairs" stuff. You can tour the house along with a tape telling you all about it. (Closed Mon, tel: 01 702 6165.)

Stroll into **Clare Street**, stopping to browse in **Greene's Bookstore** with its lovely old facade and tables of books outside.

Detour into **Kildare Street** where you find the **National Museum** where all the finest treasures of the country are displayed. There are marvelous examples of gold, bronze and other ornaments as well as relics of the Viking occupation of Dublin—the 8th-century Tara Brooch is perhaps the best known item here.

Follow the rails of Trinity College to the **Kilkenny Design Centre** and **Blarney Woolen Mills,** fine places to shop for Irish crafts and clothing.

With your back to the front gate of Trinity College, cross into **Dame Street** where the statue of Henry Grafton, a famous orator, stands with his arms outstretched outside the parliament building. Walk along Dame Street past one of Dublin's less controversial modern buildings, the **Central Bank**. The street rises slightly as you pass into what was medieval Dublin, which grew up around **Dublin Castle**, built in the early 13th century on the site of an earlier Danish fortification. The adjoining 18th-century **State**

Merrion Square

Apartments with their ornate furnishings are more impressive inside than out. (Open daily, tel: 01 677 7129.)

Returning to Dame Street you pass **City Hall** and on your right the impressive **Christ Church Cathedral** comes into view. Dedicated in 1192, it has been rebuilt and restored many times. After the Reformation when Protestant religion was imposed on the Irish people, it became a Protestant cathedral (Church of Ireland). The large crypt remained as a gathering spot and marketplace for the locals (Catholics) who used it for many years until a rector expelled them because their rowdiness was interrupting church services. Another point of interest is **Strongbow's Tomb**: he was one of the most famous kings of

Ireland and by tradition debts were paid across his tomb. When a wall collapsed and crushed the tomb a replacement, unknown crusader's tomb was conscripted and named Strongbow's Tomb. (Open daily, tel: 01 677 8099.)

Joined to the cathedral by a covered bridge that arches across the street is **Dublina** where you are guided through a visual display of the history of Dublin by a tape. You conclude your tour at the large-scale model of the city and the gift shop. (Open daily Apr–mid-Sep, tel: 01 679 4611.)

At the junction of High Street and Bridge Street, pause to climb the restored remains of a portion of **Dublin's Walls**. When they were built in 1240, the walls fronted onto the River Liffey.

If you feel like walking the distance along **Thomas Street**, now is the time to detour about 1.5 kilometers to that thriving Dublin institution, the **Guinness Brewery**, whence flows the national drink. Be aware that this is a very seedy area of town. As you near your goal the smell of roasting grains permeates the air. Entering the Guinness hop store, your reward for watching an audio-visual show on the making of the world-famous Irish brew is a sample (pints if you wish) of the divine liquid and the chance to purchase souvenirs of all things Guinness. No, the 2,000,000 gallons of water a day that the brewery uses do not come from the Liffey, but from St James's well on the Grand Canal—it is this limestone water that gives Guinness its characteristic flavor. (Open weekdays, tel: 01 453 6700, ext. 5155.)

If you are not up to the walk to the Guinness Brewery, cross diagonally from the walls to the **Brazen Head** in **Bridge Street** where you can enjoy that same brew in Dublin's oldest pub. There has been a tavern on this site since Viking times, though the present, rather dilapidated premises date from 1688. It's always a crowded spot that really comes alive late in the evening when musicians gather for impromptu traditional music sessions.

Cross the River Liffey and if you are of a macabre turn of mind, continue straight up **Church Street** to **St Michan's Church** where the crypt's interred occupants have not decomposed because the limestone walls absorb moisture from the air. This grisly spectacle can be inspected.

Strolling along the **Inns Quay** you come to **The Four Courts**, the supreme and high courts of Ireland. You can look inside the fine circular waiting hall under the beautiful green dome that allows light through its apex. If it is early morning you may see barristers in their gowns and wigs on their way to court.

Turn right up **Capel Street** and third left into **Mary Street** (a rather seedy area) where

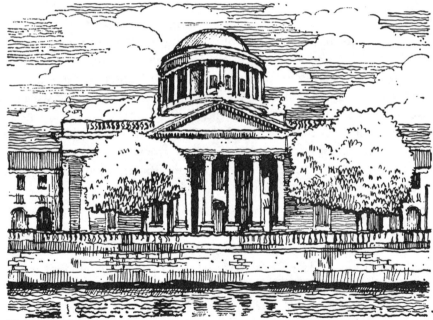

The Four Courts

little shops sell all manner of goods and lead to the busiest pedestrian shopping street in Dublin, **Henry Street**. Hardy ladies wrapped in warm woolen coats stand before their prams and bawl in Dublinese, "Bananas six for a pound" and "Peaches pound a basket." Policemen regularly move the ladies on, but within a few minutes, they are back hawking their wares.

A short detour down **Moore Street** takes you through Dublin's colorful open-air fruit, vegetable, and flower market.

On reaching **O'Connell Street** turn left. O'Connell Street has its share of tourist traps and hamburger stores, but it's a lively bunch of Dubliners who walk its promenades: placard-carrying nuns, nurses collecting for charity, hawkers of fruit, flowers, and plastic trinkets. All are there for you to see as you stroll along this wide boulevard and continue past the **Gate Theatre** into **Parnell Square** where at the north end of the square you find the **Dublin Writers Museum** in a restored 18th-century mansion. You go on a tour of the paintings and memorabilia with a tape telling you all about it. Among those featured are George Bernard Shaw, William Butler Yeats, Oscar Wilde, James Joyce, and Samuel Beckett. (Open daily, tel: 01 872 2077.) Just a few doors away is the **Hugh Lane Gallery** of modern art that ranges from works by Impressionists to contemporary Irish artists. (Closed Mon, tel: 01 874 1903.)

Retrace your steps down O'Connell Street to the **General Post Office**. The GPO, as it is affectionately known, is a national shrine as the headquarters of the 1916 revolution. Pass the statues of those who fought for Irish freedom and you are back at your starting point, the O'Connell Street Bridge.

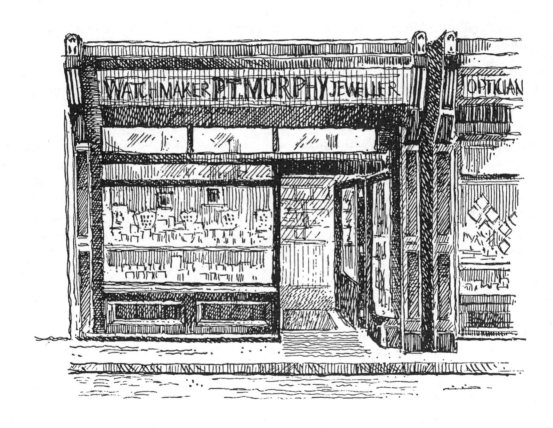

Dublin Walking Tour

The Southeast

Legend:
- ✳ Places to Stay
- ● Orientation/Sightseeing
- ▪▪▪ Itinerary Route
- — Roads
- ⋯ Alternative Route & Sidetrips
- ✈ Airport

Belfast

Dublin

✈ Dublin

Enniskerry
Powerscourt
Gardens & Waterfall
Sally Gap
Rathnew
Glendalough
Laragh
Wicklow
Vale of Avoca
Ballinaclash
Avoca
Arklow
N11

N9

Castlecomer
Bunclody
Gorey
Kilkenny
Maddoxstown
N11
Borris
Enniscorthy
Thomastown
Ballymurn
Cashel
New Ross
Bansha
Wexford
Cahir
Campile
John F. Kennedy Park
N24
Waterford
Nire Valley
Arthurstown
The Vee
Lismore
N25
Passage East
Castlelyons
Conna
Tramore
N72
Midleton
Killeagh
N25
Dungarven
Cork
N25
Youghal
Shanagarry

The Southeast

All too often visitors rush from Dublin through Waterford and on to western Ireland, never realizing that they are missing some of the most ancient antiquities and lovely scenery along the seductive little byways that traverse the moorlands and wind through wooded glens. This itinerary travels from Dublin into the Wicklow mountains, pausing to admire the lovely Powerscourt Gardens, lingering amongst the ancient monastic ruins of Glendalough, visiting the Avoca handweavers who capture the subtle hues of heather and field in their fabric, and admiring the skill of the Waterford crystal cutters.

Powerscourt Gardens

The Southeast

RECOMMENDED PACING: If you are not a leisurely sightseer, and leave Dublin early, you can follow this itinerary and be in Youghal by nightfall. But resist the temptation, select a base for two nights, and explore at leisure. If you are not continuing westward and return to Dublin via The Vee, Cashel, and Kilkenny, select a place to stay near Cashel or Kilkenny.

Leave Dublin following the N11 in the direction of Wexford. (If you experience difficulty finding the correct road, follow signs for the ferry at Dun Laoghaire and from there pick up signs for Wexford.) As soon as the city suburbs are behind you, watch for signs indicating a right turn to **Powerscourt Gardens** and **Enniskerry**. Follow the winding, wooded lane to Enniskerry and bear left in the center of the village: this brings you to the main gates of Powerscourt Gardens. As you drive through the vast, parklike grounds, the mountains of Wicklow appear before you, decked in every shade of green. Unfortunately, Powerscourt House was burnt to a ruin in 1974: a rook's nest blocked one of the chimneys, and when a fire was lit in the fireplace, the resultant blaze quickly engulfed this grand home. The gardens descend in grand tiers from the ruined house, rather as if descending into a bowl—a mirror-like lake sits at the bottom. Masses of roses adorn the walled garden and velvet, green, grassy walks lead through the woodlands. Many visitors are intrigued by the animal cemetery with its little headstones and inscriptions. Such a corner is not uncommon in Irish stately homes. (Open mid-Mar-Oct, tel: 01 286 7676.) Leaving the car park, turn left for the 6-kilometer drive to the foot of **Powerscourt Waterfall**, the highest waterfall in Ireland and a favorite summer picnic place for many Dubliners.

Turn to the left as you leave the waterfall grounds to meander along narrow country lanes towards **Glencree**. As you come upon open moorland, take the first turn left for the 8-kilometer uphill drive to the summit of **Sally Gap**. This road is known as the old military road because it follows the path that the British built across these wild mountains to aid them in their attempts to suppress the feisty men of County Wicklow. Neat stacks of turf are piled to dry in the sun and the wind. Grazing sheep seem to be the only occupants of this vast, rolling moorland. Below **Glenmacnass Waterfall** the valley opens up to a patchwork of fields beckoning you to **Laragh** and Glendalough

Glendalough was founded by St Kevin in the 6th century—a monastic settlement of seven churches. After St Patrick, St Kevin is Ireland's most popular saint. He certainly picked a stunning site in this wooded valley between two lakes to found his monastic order. Amidst the tilting stones of the graveyard, the round tower punctuates the skyline—still perfect after more than a thousand years. Guided tours and illustrated lectures on the history of the area and of monastic architecture are conducted at the Interpretive Centre. (Open all year, tel: 0404 45325.) Leaving the monastery, continue up the narrow road until it dead-ends at the Upper Lake. Tradition has it that St Kevin lived a solitary life in a hut near here. Farther up on a cliff face is a cave known as St Kevin's Bed. Here, so the story goes, Kathleen, a beautiful temptress, tried to seduce St Kevin. To cool her advances, he threw her into the lake.

Retrace the road to Laragh, turn right, and travel south through Rathdrum. Two miles beyond Rathdrum a left turn brings you to **Avondale House**, the home of Charles Stewart Parnell. The house has been restored and contains Parnell memorabilia. You can also wander around the estate with its wonderful trees. (Open May-Sep daily, Oct-Apr weekends, tel: 0404 46111.)

Travel through the **Vale of Avoca** to the "Meeting of the Waters" at the confluence of the rivers Avonmore and Avonbeg. Detour into **Avoca** to visit the **Avoca Handweavers**. You are welcome to wander amongst the skeins and bobbins of brightly-hued wool to see the weavers at work and talk to them above the noise of the looms. An adjacent shop sells tweeds and woolens.

At **Arklow** join the N11, a broad, fast road taking you south through Gorey and Ferns to **Enniscorthy**. Amidst the gray stone houses built on steeply sloping ground by the River Slaney lies a Norman castle. Rebuilt in 1586, the castle houses a folk museum that includes exhibits from the Stone Age to the present day, with the emphasis on the part

Glendalough

played by local people in the 1798 rebellion against English rule. (Open all year, tel: 054 35926.)

Before reaching **New Ross** the N79 merges with the N25 where you turn left for Arthurstown and the **John F. Kennedy Park**. The great-grandfather of American President John F. Kennedy emigrated from nearby Dunganstown, driven from Ireland by the terrible potato famine of the 1840s. Row upon row of dark evergreens stand before you like an honor guard to the slain president as you climb to the panoramic viewing point atop Slieve Coillte. (Open all year, tel: 051 88171.)

Return to the main road and continue south to **Arthurstown** where the **Passage East Ferry** takes you across the estuary to **Passage East**, the tiny village on the western shores of Waterford harbor. Arriving at the N25, you turn right to visit the town of **Waterford** fronting the River Suir, and left to arrive at **Waterford Crystal Factory**. If you do not have an appointment you can see the hand-blowing and cutting of sparkling crystal on a video presentation. The adjacent showroom displays the full line of Waterford's production from shimmering chandeliers to glassware. There are no seconds and Waterford crystal items are uniformly priced throughout the country. Tours are offered on weekdays five times a day from 10:15 am to 2:30 pm by appointment only. The factory is closed most of August, tel: 051 74531.

From the factory, double back in the direction of Waterford for a very short distance, turning to the right to **Tramore**, a family holiday town, long a favorite of the "ice-cream-and-bucket-and-spade brigade." Skirting the town, follow the beautiful coastal road through **Annestown** to **Dungarven**.

Where the coastal road meets the N25, make a detour from your route turning sharp left to **Shell House**—like it or hate it, there is nothing quite like it on any suburban street in the world—a cottage where all available wall surfaces are decorated with colored shells in various patterns. Ring the bell to tour the garden and you will probably be invited in to view shell souvenirs. Their sale aids leper colonies in Africa and their purchase certainly celebrates the ingenuity that went into creating the yard.

Returning to the main road after crossing Dungarven harbor, the N25 winds up and away from the coast, presenting lovely views of the town and the coast. If you haven't eaten, try **Seanachie** (a restored thatched farmhouse, now a traditional restaurant and bar) which sits atop the hill and serves good Irish and Continental food.

After passing through several kilometers of forests, turn left on the R673 to **Ardmore**, following the coastline to the village. Beyond the neatly-painted houses that cluster together, lies the **Ardmore Monastic Site**. The well-preserved round tower used to have six internal timber landings which were joined by ladders, and at the top was a bell to call the monks to prayer or warn of a hostile raid. The round tower is unique to Ireland, its entrance door placed well above the ground: entry was gained by means of a ladder which could be drawn up whenever necessary. Early Christian monks built round towers as protection against Vikings and other raiders.

Leaving the ruins, turn left in the village for **Youghal** where this itinerary ends. Sightseeing in Youghal is outlined in the following itinerary. From Youghal you can continue west to follow the *Southwest* itinerary, or take the following alternative route back to Dublin via the Vee, Cashel, and Kilkenny.

Youghal

ROUTE FROM YOUGHAL TO DUBLIN VIA THE VEE, CASHEL, AND KILKENNY

From Youghal retrace your steps towards Waterford to the bridge that crosses the River Blackwater and turn sharp left (before you cross the river) on **Blackwater Valley Drive**, a narrow road which follows the broad, muddy waters of the Blackwater through scenic wooded countryside. The "drive" is well signposted as Scenic Route. Quiet country roads bring you into **Lismore**. Turn left into town and right at the town square. Cross the river and take the second road to the left, following signs for **Clogheen** and **The Vee**. As the road climbs, woods give way to heathery moorlands climbing to the summit where the valley opens before you—a broad "V" shape framing an endless patchwork of fields in every shade of green.

Continue on to **Cahir Castle** that has stood on guard to defend the surrounding town of **Cahir** since 1375. A guided tour explains the elaborate defensive system, making a visit here both interesting and informative. A separate audio-visual presentation provides information about the castle and other monuments in the area. (Open Oct-May, closed Mon, tel: 052 41011.)

Leaving the castle, continue through the town square for the 16-kilometer drive to **Cashel**. The **Rock of Cashel** seems to grow out of the landscape as you near the town and you can see why this easily defensible site was the capital for the kings of Munster as long ago as 370 AD. In the course of converting Ireland to Christianity, St Patrick reached the castle and, according to legend, jabbed his staff into the king's foot during the conversion ceremony. The king apparently took it all very stoically, thinking it was part of the ritual. Upon reaching the summit of the rock, you find a 10th-century round tower, a 13th-century cathedral, and a 15th-century entrance building or Hall of Vicars Choral, a building that was sensitively restored in the 1970s and now houses some exhibits including St Patrick's Cross, an ancient Irish high cross of unusual design. (Open all year, tel: 062 61437.)

Leave Cashel on the N8 for the 40-kilometer drive northeast to **Urlingford** where you bear right for the 27-kilometer drive to **Kilkenny**. Kilkenny is quite the loveliest of Irish towns and it is easy to spend a day here sightseeing and shopping. Entering the town, turn left at the first traffic lights along the main street and park your car outside the castle.

Kilkenny Castle was first built between 1195 and 1207. The imposing building as it now stands is a mixture of Tudor and Gothic design and is definitely worth a visit. The east wing picture gallery is flooded by natural light from the skylights in the roof and displays a collection of portraits of the Ormonde family, the owners of Kilkenny Castle from 1391 until 1967. (Open all year, tel: 056 21450.)

Opposite the castle entrance, the stables now house the **Kilkenny Design Centre**, a retail outlet for goods of Irish design and production: silver jewelry, knits, textiles, furniture, and crafts.

Undoubtedly the best way to see the medieval buildings of Kilkenny is on foot. A walking tour starts from the Tourist Office in the **Shee Alms House** just a short distance from the castle. Stroll up High Street into Parliament Street to **Rothe House**. The house, built in 1594 as the home of Elizabethan merchant John Rothe, is now a museum depicting how such a merchant lived. You should also see **St Canice's Cathedral** at the top of Parliament Street. The round tower dates from the 6th century when St Canice founded a monastic order here. Building began on the cathedral in 1251, though most of the lovely church you see today is an 1864 restoration.

Alleyways with fanciful names such as The Butter Slip lead you from the High Street to St Kieran Street where you find **Kylters Inn,** the oldest building in town. This historic inn has a lurid history—supposedly a hostess of many centuries ago murdered four successive husbands, was then accused of witchcraft, and narrowly escaped being burnt at the stake by fleeing to the Continent.

A 100-kilometer drive along the N10 and N9 returns you to Dublin.

Rock of Cashel

The Southwest

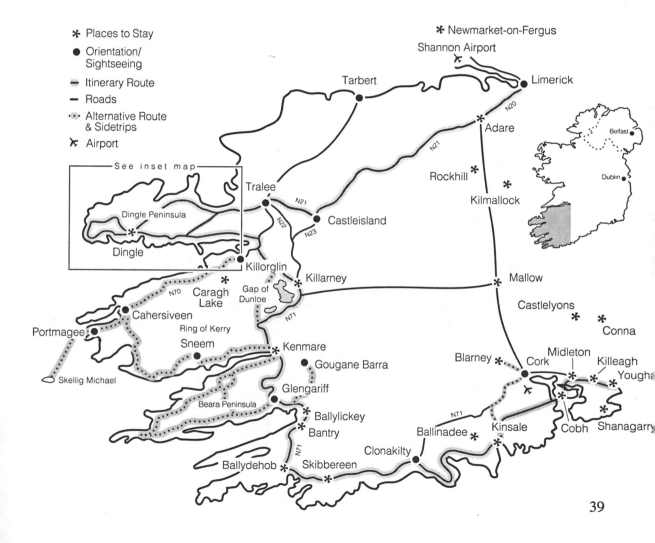

Legend:
- ✳ Places to Stay
- ● Orientation/Sightseeing
- ▬ Itinerary Route
- ━ Roads
- ⋯ Alternative Route & Sidetrips
- ✈ Airport

See inset map

✳ Newmarket-on-Fergus
Shannon Airport
Limerick
Tarbert
Adare
N20
Rockhill
N21
Kilmallock
Belfast
Dublin
Tralee
N21
Castleisland
N22
N23
Dingle Peninsula
Dingle
Killorglin
Killarney
Mallow
Gap of Dunloe
Caragh Lake
N70
Castlelyons
Cahersiveen
N71
Conna
Portmagee
Ring of Kerry
Sneem
Blarney
Midleton
Killeagh
Youghal
Skellig Michael
Kenmare
Cork
Gougane Barra
Shanagarry
Glengariff
Beara Peninsula
Ballylickey
Kinsale
Cobh
Bantry
Ballinadee
N71
Ballydehob
Skibbereen
Clonakilty
N71

The Southwest

The scenery of the southwest is absolutely magnificent: the mellow charm of Kinsale Harbor, the rugged gorges that wind you towards Glengariff and its island filled with subtropical vegetation, the translucent lakes of Killarney, and the ever-changing light on spectacular seascapes on the Dingle Peninsula. Relish the fabled beauties of this lovely part of Ireland. Take time to detour to Blarney to take part in the tradition of climbing atop Blarney Castle to kiss the stone that is said to confer "the gift of the gab." Do not hurry: allow time to linger over breakfast, enjoy a chat over a glass of Guinness, sample freshly caught salmon and scallops, and join in an evening singsong in a local pub.

Dingle

RECOMMENDED PACING: For this portion of the itinerary select a location near the southern coast, one in either Kenmare or Killarney, and one in Dingle. Allow one or two nights in each spot.

Your journey to the Southwest begins in **Youghal** (pronounced yawl). Sir Walter Raleigh, who introduced the potato and tobacco from the New World, was once its mayor. It's a pleasant old town, dominated by the clock tower which was built in 1776 and served as the town's jail. The one-way traffic system makes it impossible to explore without parking the car and walking. Several of the Main Street shops have been refurbished, but the town still has an "ungussied-up" look to it. Make your first stop the **Heritage Centre** with its displays on the town, where you can pick up a brochure that outlines a walking tour of the old buildings.

Traveling the A25, a 30-kilometer drive brings you to the heart of **Midleton** where you find the **Jameson Heritage Centre** in the old whiskey distillery. Marvel at the world's largest pot distillery in the courtyard (capacity 143,872 liters), learn about whiskey production, visit the huge waterwheel, and be rewarded by a sample of the golden liquor. There's also a shop and cafe. (Open Mar-Oct, tel: 021 631821.)

Just before you reach Cork, turn left for Cobh. **Fota House**, situated on a small island in Cork harbor, is popular with locals who come to picnic in its grounds and enjoy its wildlife park. The house has been restored by the University of Cork. Its interior is decorated in bright tones with daylight streaming through the skylights and tall windows. There's a repeated motif of a Greek vase and regency-style plaster panels that give the house great style. A collection of Irish landscape paintings hangs on the walls. (Open all year, tel: 021 812555.)

Nearby **Cobh** (pronounced cove) was renamed Queenstown to mark the visit of Queen Victoria in 1849 and reverted back to Cobh in 1922. There's a long tradition of naval operations here, as its large harbor is a safe anchorage. The **Cobh Experience**, an audio-visual display housed in the restored Victorian railway station, tells the story of this port.

Cobh was the point of departure for many emigrants, off to seek a better life in America and Australia. For many it was the last piece of Irish soil they stood on before taking a boat to a new life. The ill-fated *Lusitania* was torpedoed not far from Cobh and survivors were brought here. It was also the last port of call of the *Titanic*. There's an excellent shop and cafe—an enjoyable place to spend a couple of hours on a rainy day. (Closed January, tel: 021 813591, fax: 021 813595.)

Retrace your steps a short distance to the **Carriagaloe-Glenbrook ferry** which transports you across Cork harbor and eliminates the hassle of driving through Cork city. A short countryside drive brings you to **Kinsale**, its harbor full of tall-masted boats. Narrow, winding streets lined both with quaint and several sadly derelict houses lead up from the harbor. Flowers abound: small posies tucked into little baskets, spilling from windowboxes, are artistically planted at every turn. As well as for its floral extravaganza, Kinsale is noted as being the gourmet capital of Ireland. A group of twelve restaurants have come together to form a good food circle. It's a pleasant pastime to check some of the menus on display as you inhale mouth-watering aromas and peek at happy people enjoying their food.

There has been a fortress in Kinsale since Norman times. A great battle nearby in 1601 precipitated the flight of the earls and sounded the death knell of the ancient Gaelic civilization. It was from Kinsale that James II left for exile after his defeat at Boyne Water. Bypassed by 20th-century events, Kinsale has emerged as a village full of character, attracting visitors who find themselves seduced by its charms.

About 3 kilometers east of Kinsale, the impressive, 17th-century **Charles Fort** stands guard over the entrance to its harbor. It takes several hours to tour the five bastions that make up the complex. The ordnance sheds are restored and hold a photographic and historical exhibition about the fort. (Open Apr-Sep, tel: 021 772236.)

The Southwest

Kinsale

Across the estuary you see the 1603 **James Fort,** where William Penn's father was governor of Kinsale, while William worked as a clerk of the Admiralty Court. Later William was given a land grant in America on which he founded the state of Pennsylvania.

SIDE TRIP TO BLARNEY

*About a half-hour drive north of Kinsale lies **Blarney Castle** and its famous tourist attraction, the **Blarney Stone.** Kissing the Blarney Stone, by climbing atop the keep and hanging upside-down is said to confer the "gift of the gab." Even if you are not inclined to join in this back-breaking, unhygienic pursuit, the castle is worth a visit. (Open all* *year, tel: 021 385252.)* **Blarney Castle House** *next door has been home to the Colhurst family for over a hundred years and they open up their doors in the afternoon to visitors. The light, airy rooms are furnished in exquisite taste. (Open Jun-Sep, closed Sun, tel: 021 385252.) Just up the street,* **Blarney Woolen Mills** *is an excellent place to shop for all things Irish, particularly knitwear.*

Leave Kinsale along the harbor, cross the Bandon River, and follow country lanes to the sleepy little village of **Ballinspittle**. As you drive through the village, it is hard to imagine that in 1985 it was overwhelmed by pilgrims. They came to the village shrine after a local girl reported seeing the statue of the Virgin Mary rocking back and forth. You pass the shrine on your right just before you come to the village.

Follow country lanes to **Timoleague**, a very small coastal village watched over by the ruins of a Franciscan abbey and on to the N71 and **Clonakilty** and **Skibbereen**. As you travel westwards rolling fields in every shade of green present themselves.

Arriving at the waterfront in **Bantry,** you come to **The Bantry 1796 French Armada Centre** that retells the story of the French Armada which tried to invade Ireland in 1796. It failed and a model of one of the armada's ships that sank in Bantry Bay is on display—a very interesting look at a little-known piece of Irish history.

Next door is **Bantry House**. Like so many other Irish country houses, it has seen better days, but the present owner, Egerton Shelswell-White, makes visitors welcome and gives a typed information sheet, in the language of your choice, that guides you room-by-room through the house. The house has a wonderful collection of pictures, furniture, and works of art, brought together by the second Earl of Bantry during his European travels during the first half of the 19th century. In contrast to his ancestors' staid portraits, Egerton is shown playing his trombone. (Open all year, tel: 027 50047.)

Apart from furnishing the house, the second Earl, inspired by the gardens of Europe, laid out a formal Italian garden and a "staircase to the sky" rising up the steep terraces to the crest of the hill behind the house. If you are not up to the climb, you can still enjoy a magnificent, though less lofty view across the boat-filled bay from the terrace in front of the house. A very pleasant tea and gift shop occupies the old kitchen. One wing of the house has been renovated and modernized to provide upmarket bed-and-breakfast accommodation—see listing. Eight kilometers north lies **Ballylickey**.

SIDE TRIP TO GOUGANE BARRA LAKE

*From Ballylickey an inland excursion takes you to **Gougane Barra Lake**, a beautiful lake locked into a ring of mountains. Here you find a small hotel where you can stop for a snack or a warming drink, and a little church on an island in the lake, the oratory where St Finbarr went to contemplate and pray. The road to and from the lake takes you over a high pass and through mountain tunnels.*

As you drive through **Glengariff** various boatmen will hail you to select their boat for a 10-minute ride to Garinish Island. Do not be put off by their good-natured banter, for it is a most worthwhile trip.

Garinish Island, once a barren rock where only gorse and heather grew, was transformed into a miniature botanical paradise at the beginning of this century by a Scottish politician, Arran Bryce. The sheltered site of the island provides perfect growing conditions for trees, shrubs, and flowers from all over the world. It took a hundred men over three years to sculpt this lovely spot with its formal Italian garden, caseta, and temple. (Open Mar-Oct, closed Sat, tel: 027 63081.)

From Glengariff the road winds upwards, and glancing behind, you have a spectacular view of **Bantry Bay** lying beyond a patchwork of green fields. Rounding the summit, the road tunnels through a large buttress of rock and you emerge to stunning views of sparse rocky hillsides.

Cross the River Kenmare into **Kenmare**. This pleasant town of gray, stone houses, with gaily painted shop fronts lining two broad main streets, is a summer favorite with tourists who prefer its peace and charm to the hectic pace of Killarney. It is a perfect place for exploring both the Iveragh (Ring of Kerry) and Beara peninsulas. It also serves as a stepping-off point for a side trip to Skellig Michael.

SIDE TRIP TO THE BEARA PENINSULA

*If you do not stop along the way, it will take you between two and three hours to drive the **Beara Peninsula** where the scenery is wild, but gorgeous. From Kenmare a minor road (R571) takes you along the north shore of the peninsula to **Ardgroom**, a picturesque village that nestles beside a little harbor at the foot of the mountains. Farther west, **Eyeries** village looks out over the Skellig Rocks and several rocky inlets. Behind the village, the mountain road rises up through the Pass of Boffickle for a fantastic view back over the bay. In the 19th century **Allihies** was a center of the copper-mining industry, but now it is a resort with a magnificent beach curving along the bay. At the most westerly point of the peninsula lies **Garinish** where a cable car takes visitors over to **Dursey Island**.*

Dursey is a long, mountain island encircled by high cliffs. Offshore are a number of other islands, the most interesting of which is Bull Rock, a roosting place for gannets. A cave passes right through it, creating a massive rock arch.

*Skirting the southern shore of the peninsula, the narrow road hugs the ocean through **Castletownbere** and **Adrigole** from where you can follow the coastal road into **Glengariff** or take the opportunity for a spectacular view by turning left and ascending the **Healy Pass**. It's hard to turn and admire the vista of **Bantry Bay** as the road gently zigzags up the pass, so stop at the top to relish the view before continuing down to **Lauraugh,** where you turn right for Kenmare.*

SIDE TRIP TO IVERAGH PENINSULA—RING OF KERRY

Rather than follow the itinerary you can use The Ring of Kerry as a route to Dingle or Killarney.

*The drive round the **Iveragh Peninsula** is, in my opinion, highly overrated, but if you want to see the much-publicized **Ring of Kerry**, hope that the fickle Irish weather is at its best, for when mists wreathe the Ring it takes a lot of imagination to conjure up seascapes as you drive down fog-shrouded lanes. Even if the weather is dull, do not lose heart, because at any moment the sun could break through. Driving the ring can be a trial during the busy summer months when the roads are choked with tourist coaches.*

*Beginning the Ring, a pleasant drive takes you along the Kenmare River estuary and you get tempting glimpses of water and the Beara Peninsula. Arriving at **Sneem** enjoy the most picturesque village on the Ring, with its tiny, gaily-painted houses bordering two village greens. The most beautiful scenery on the Ring of Kerry (the largest of the three western peninsulas) lies between Sneem and **Waterville**. Rounding the peninsula you come to **Cahersiveen,** a classic Irish town with a long main street made up of shops and pubs. Concluding the ring, a pleasant drive across wild moorlands takes you to **Killorglin**. However, our suggested route for your return to Kenmare is to take a right hand turn to **Caragh Lake** (5 kilometers before your reach Killorglin) and follow the narrow lanes around this beautiful lake and across the rugged McGillcuddy Reeks (Ireland's highest mountains) to Blackwater Bridge (on the Ring) and Kenmare—a trip only to be undertaken on a clear day.*

View to Little Skellig from Skellig Michael

SIDE TRIP TO SKELLIG MICHAEL

*The trip to **Skellig Michael** cannot be counted upon until the actual day because it depends on the seas being calm. Few boats are government-licensed to make the trip to Skellig Michael. I was very comfortable with the arrangements I made with Des Lavelle who has served with the local lifeboat, written an authoritative book on Skellig Michael, and operates a scuba diving school. His boat leaves from **Valencia Island**, stopping to pick up passengers in **Portmagee**. (Operates Easter-Oct, Sun, Mon, Tue—book 2 days ahead, tel: 066 76124, fax: 066 76309.) Remember to wear flat-heeled shoes and take a waterproof jacket, an extra sweater, and lunch. The morning departure for the island and the late afternoon return necessitate your spending two nights on the Ring of Kerry. The nearest accommodation recommendations in this guide are Caragh Lake and Kenmare which are too long a drive for all but the earliest riser. You might want to consider spending the night prior to your trip with Des and Pat Lavelle at their simple* *bed and breakfast,* **Lavelle's**, *which is adjacent to the boat dock on Valencia Island. (Open Easter-Oct, tel: 066 76124, fax: 066 76309.)*

Skellig Michael is a very special place, a rocky island topped by the ruins of an ancient monastery lying 12 kilometers off the coast of the Ring of Kerry. Arriving at the cove beneath the looming rock, the first part of your ascent follows the path to the abandoned lighthouse, past seabirds' nests clinging to tiny crevasses in the steep rock slopes. Rounding a corner, the monks' stairway appears and it's up hundreds and hundreds of hand-hewn stone steps to the monastery perched on a ledge high above the pounding ocean. Pausing to catch your breath, you wonder at the monks who set out in fragile little boats to establish this monastery and toiled with crude implements to build these steps up the sheer rock face.

At the summit six little beehive huts, a slightly larger stone oratory, and the roofless walls of a small church nestle against the hillside, some poised at the edge—only a low stone wall between them and the churning ocean far below. The windowless interiors of the huts hardly seem large enough for a person to lie down. Remarkably, the monks' only water source was rainwater runoff stored in rock fissures.

It is reputed that the monks arrived in 600AD. According to annals, the Vikings raided in 812AD and 823AD and found an established community. It is documented that the last monks departed in the 13th century. When it is time to leave this spot there is a sense of wonder at the men who toiled in this rocky place, enduring deprivation, hardship, and solitude to achieve a state of grace. The Office of Public Works is maintaining and restoring the site and there may be someone to impart information.

As a complement (or an alternative) to visiting Skellig Michael visit the **Skellig Heritage Centre** *on Valencia Island. The center is found where the roadbridge meets the island, directly opposite Portmagee. An audio-visual presentation, "The Call of the Skelligs," takes you to the Skellig Michael monastery while displays show the bird and sealife of the islands. (Open Apr-Sep, tel: 0667 6306.)*

Ladies' View, Killarney

From Kenmare travel over one of Ireland's most beautiful roads (N71) for the 34 kilometer drive over the hills to **Killarney**, stopping at **Ladies' View** to admire a spectacular panorama with the lakes of Killarney spread at your feet.

In amongst the woodlands you find the car park for **Torc Waterfall**. Following the stream, a short uphill walk brings you to the celebrated 20-meter cascade of water.

Muckross House and Gardens is 5 kilometers out of Killarney on the Kenmare road. Leave your car outside the lower entrance to the estate and hire a horse and trap to take you through the grounds alongside the lake to the house and gardens or, if you prefer, you can take one of the lovely walks that bring you to the house. (A second entrance, farther down the Kenmare road, gives access to a car park adjacent to the house.) Muckross House was built in 1843 in Tudor style. Much of the interior is furnished in a

Victorian manner and the remainder of the house serves as a folk museum with various exhibits. There is also a blacksmith, potter, gift shop, and tea room. The gardens surrounding the house contain many subtropical plants. (Open Nov-Mar, closed Mon, tel: 064 31440.)

Believe everything you ever read about the magnificent beauty of the Killarney lakes, but realize that Killarney town is absolutely packed with tourists during the summer season. If you would like additional views of the lakes, then a tour to Aghadoe Hill or a boat trip from Ross Castle should give you what you are looking for. Leave Killarney on the road to Tralee (N22) and turn left for the 5-kilometer drive to **Aghadoe** where Killarney town, lakes, and mountains can all be seen from this vantage point. If you prefer a close look at the lake and its island, take the 90-minute boat tour of the Lower Lake which leaves from the jetty alongside the ruin of **Ross Castle**. Tickets for this trip can be purchased from the Tourist Office in town.

SIDE TRIP UP THE GAP OF DUNLOE

*If you are in the mood for an evening adventure (this is not a trip that should be attempted on a wet, rainsoaked evening), you can drive through the beautiful **Gap of Dunloe** and emerge back on the road to Killarney just west of **Moll's Gap**. If you decide to drive, you must wait until after seven in the evening as the daytime horse traffic on this narrow, unpaved road will not let you pass! Leave Killarney on the Killorglin road and after passing the golf course make a left-hand turn at the signpost for the Gap of Dunloe.*

*Kate Kearney's Cottage is at the entrance to the ravine. Legend has it that Kate was a beautiful witch who drove men wild with desire. Now her home is greatly enlarged as a coffee and souvenir shop. Beyond the cottage the road continues as a single-lane dirt track up a 6-kilometer ravine carved by glaciers. The dramatic setting is enhanced by the purple mountains on your left and **Macgillicuddy's Reeks** on you right. As you drive up the gorge, the walls rise ever steeper and you pass deep glacial lakes—the farther you* *travel into the gap, the more you are moved by its haunting beauty. Cresting the ravine, the track winds down into another valley and becomes a single-lane, paved road with passing places that joins the N71 to the west of the narrow passage through the rocks known as Moll's Gap. Following the road back into town, you come to* **Ladies' View,** *which on a clear evening offers unparalleled views of the lakes of Killarney. From here you return to Killarney.*

THE DINGLE PENINSULA

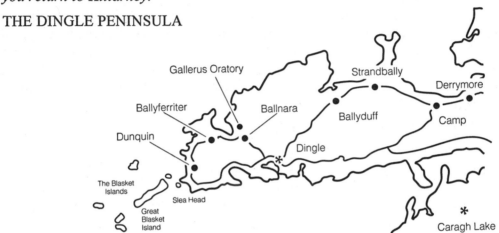

Leaving Killarney, a two-hour drive will bring you to Limerick but, rather than taking a direct route, take the time to explore the lovely **Dingle Peninsula**. It's a very special place, a narrow promontory of harshly beautiful land and seascapes where the people are especially friendly and welcoming to strangers. The road from Killarney to Dingle town takes you northwest to **Castlemaine** where you follow the coast road west through Inch to the pub-lined main street of **Dingle** town, the largest settlement on the peninsula. The occasional windowbox brightens the plain, gray houses and fishing boats bob in the harbor unloading bountiful catches of fish and shellfish. It is not surprising that you find a great many excellent seafood restaurants here. Its population is under 2,000 yet it has over 50 pubs, some of which double as shops so you can buy a pair of shoes while enjoying a cold drink. The town has many fish restaurants—**The Half Door** and adjacent **Doyle's** are two upmarket favorites. After dinner ask where you can go to hear traditional Irish music.

While the road distance is short (it's only an hour-and-a-half drive from Dingle to Killarney), it would be a pity not to experience the beauty and tranquillity offered by the unspoiled scenery of the spectacular beaches and rocky promontories that lie to the west of Dingle town. Plan to spend at least two nights on the peninsula to take the trip to the Blasket Islands, and afford time to wander along the beaches or walk along the hedgerow-lined lanes dividing the fields where friendly locals pause from their work to call a greeting and wave a salute of welcome.

The road to Slea Head twists and turns, following the contours of the increasingly rocky coast. Stunning seascapes present themselves, demanding that you pause just to admire the view. Several of the farms along the way have beehive stone huts and for a small fee the farmers will let you climb up to visit them. A large white crucifix marks **Slea Head** which affords the first view of the **Blasket Islands**—alternately sparkling like jewels in the blue ocean and disappearing under dark clouds a moment later.

Around the point you come to the scattered village of **Dunquin** and the **Blasket Island Centre**. The building is impressive with exhibits lining a long corridor that leads to an observatory overlooking the island's abandoned village. Remarkably this tiny, isolated island abode produced an outpouring of music, and especially writing. Three classics of Irish literature emerged with Peig Sayers' *Peig*, Thomas Crohan's *The Islandman*, and Maurice O'Sullivan's *Twenty Years a'Growing*. The islands have been uninhabited since 1953 when the last islanders evacuated their windswept home. The large airy dining room serves tempting food and provides enticing island views. (Open all year, tel: 066 56444.)

Dunquin's pier sits away from the scattered village and is reached by a steep path that zigzags down the cliff. As you round the last twist you see curraghs turned upside down looking like giant black beetles stranded high above the water line. Curraghs are fragile boats made of tarred canvas stretched over a wooden skeleton. St Brendon is reputed to have discovered America in such a boat. In clear weather a ferry takes day-trip visitors to and from **Great Blasket Island**. The little village on the island is mostly in ruins and paths wander amongst the fields where the hardy islanders struggled to earn a living—a cafe offers the only shelter. (Ferry sails every hour 10 am to 6 pm in summer, tel: 066 56455.)

Over 1,000 years ago many of St Brendan's contemporaries lived on the Dingle Peninsula in unmortared, beehive-shaped stone huts called clochans. The most famous example is the **Gallerus Oratory**, a tiny church built not as a circle, but in the shape of an upturned boat. It has a small window at one end, a small door at the other, and is as watertight today as when it was built over 900 years ago. (The oratory is located beyond **Ballyferriter**.) From here the road takes you south to **Ballnara, Milltown**, and back to Dingle.

Leaving the Dingle Peninsula (signpost Tralee) the **Connor Pass** twists you upward to the summit where a backward glance gives you a magnificent view of Dingle and its harbor. The view is spectacular, but there is no guarantee that you will see it. All will be green fields and blue sea and sky, until the mists roll in and everything vanishes.

Follow the coast road through **Ballyduff, Strandbally**, and **Camp** to **Tralee**. (If you are heading for the Cliffs of Moher take the N69 to the **Tarbert Ferry** which takes you across the River Shannon.) At Tralee you join the main road (N21) for the drive to **Castleisland** and on to **Adare** with its charming row of thatched cottages, and tree-lined streets. Less than an hour's drive will find you in **Limerick** whose traffic-crowded streets can be avoided by taking the ring-road signposted Ennis and Shannon Airport.

The West

Céide Fields

Sligo

Bangor

N59

* Riverstown

* Ballymote

Crossmolina

Ballina

Lough Conn

N17

Achill Island

Mulrany

Newport

Rosturk

Castlebar

* Knock

N59

* Westport

Ballintubber Abbey

Louisburgh

Inishbofin Island

N59

Leenane

Lough Mask

Cleggan

Cong

Kingstown

Letterfrack

Lough Corrib

Clifden

Cashel

Oughterard

Aughnanure Castle

Roundstone

Moycullen

N59

Rosaveel

Galway

Dunguaire Castle

Aran Islands

Kilronan

Dun Aengus

Lisdoonvarna

Ballyvaughan

Thoor Ballylee

The Burren

Kilfenora

N18

Corofin

Ennis

Clarecastle

* Newmarket-on-Fergus

Shannon Airport

Limerick

Belfast

Dublin

* Places to Stay

● Orientation/ Sightseeing

━ Itinerary Route

━ Roads

┅ Alternative Route & Sidetrips

✈ Airport

55

The West

This itinerary takes you off the beaten tourist track through the wild, hauntingly beautiful scenery of County Clare, Connemara, and County Mayo. Lying on the coast of County Clare, the Burren presents a vast landscape of smooth limestone rocks whose crevices are ablaze with rock roses, blue gentians, and all manner of Arctic and Alpine flowers in the spring and early summer. Otherwise there are no trees, shrubs, rivers, or lakes—just bare moonscapes of rocks dotted with forts and ruined castles, tombs, and rock cairns. Traveling to Connemara, your route traces the vast, island-dotted Lough Corrib and traverses boglands and moorlands. Distant mountains fill the horizon and guide you to the coast where gentle waves lap at rocky inlets sheltering scattered villages, and whitewashed cottages dot the landscape. Ireland's holy mountain, Croagh Patrick, and the windswept Achill Island leave a deep impression on the visitor.

Cliffs of Moher

RECOMMENDED PACING: It is possible to tour the west in just a few days, but this beautiful area calls for you to linger. Our ideal would be one or two nights on or near the Burren, two or three nights in Connemara, and two or three nights near either Crossmolina or Sligo.

Leave **Limerick** in the direction of Ennis and Shannon Airport and you soon arrive at **Bunratty Castle and Folk Park**. An interesting history and guide to the castle is available at the entrance. As the majority of castles in Ireland stand roofless and in ruins, it is a treat to visit a 15th-century castle that has been restored so beautifully. The authentic 14th- to 17th-century furniture in the rooms gives the castle a really lived-in feel. In the evenings firelit banquets, warmed with goblets of mead, whisk visitors back to the days when the castle was young. In the castle grounds a folk park contains several cottages, farmhouses, and a whole 19th-century village street of shops, houses and buildings furnished appropriately for their era. The community is brought to life by costumed townspeople who cook, make candles, thatch, and farm. (Open all year, tel: 061 61511.) **Bunratty Cottage**, opposite the castle, offers a wide range of handmade Irish goods, and just at the entrance to the park is **Durty Nelly's**, one of Ireland's most popular pubs, dating from the 1600s.

Just to the northwest lies the strangest landscape in Ireland, the **Burren**. Burren means "a rocky place" and this is certainly the case for as far as the eye can see this is a wilderness. A wilderness that is rich in archaeological sights (megalithic tombs, ring forts, and the remains of ancient huts) and strange rock formations whose tiny crevices are a mass of Arctic, Mediterranean, and Alpine flowers in springtime. Ludlow, one of Cromwell's generals, passing through the area in 1649, wrote, "There is not enough wood to hang a man, nor water to drown him, nor earth enough to bury him in."

Base yourself at either **Corofin** or **Ballyvaughan** (see *Places to Stay*) to explore this unique area. To help you appreciate this unusual landscape, first visit the **Burren Display Centre** at **Kilfenora** which offers a 15-minute lecture and 10-minute film on the geology and rare flora and fauna of the area. Models explain the pattern of settlement and the geological makeup of the area and silk flowers show the non-botanist what to look for. Next to the display center an old churchyard contains some interesting high crosses with symbolic carvings. (Open Mar-Oct, tel: 065 88030.)

Turn right as you leave the interpretive center and left as you come to the main road to reach the **Cliffs of Moher,** the most spectacular section of the coastline, where towering cliffs rise above the pounding Atlantic Ocean. These majestic cliffs stretching along 5 kilometers of the coast are one of Ireland's most popular sights. The cliffs face due west which means that the best time to see them is on a bright summer evening. The visitors' center offers welcome shelter on cool and windy days. (Open all year, tel: 065 81171.) A short distance from the visitors' center, **O'Brien's Tower** (built in 1835 by Sir Cornelius O'Brien, member of parliament, for "strangers visiting the magnificent scenery of this neighborhood") marks the highest and most photographed point along the clifftops.

On leaving the cliffs, head north towards, but not into, Lisdoonvarna and follow the coastal road around Black Head where the rocky Burren spills into Galway Bay to Ballyvaughan where you turn right following signs for the **Ailwee Caves** on the bluff above you. The visitors' center is so cleverly designed that it is hard to distinguish it from the surrounding gray landscape. Beneath the eerie moonscape of the Burren lie vast caves, streams, and lakes. You can take a tour through a small section of these underground caverns. The first cave is called Bear Haven because the bones of a brown bear who died long ago were found here. In other chambers you see limestone cascades, stalactites, and stalagmites before the tour ends at the edge of an underground river. Remember to dress warmly, for it's cool in the caves. (Open Mar-Nov, tel: 065 77036.)

Retrace your steps a short distance down the road towards Ballyvaughan and take the first turn left, passing Gregans Castle hotel and up Corkscrew Hill, a winding road that takes you from a lush green valley to the gray, rocky landscape above. Take the first turn to the left and you come to **Cahermacnaghter,** a ring fort that was occupied until the

18th century. It is entered via a medieval, two-story gateway, and the foundations of similar-date buildings can be seen inside the stone wall.

Some 7 kilometers farther south, you come to another ring fort, **Ballykinvarga**. You have to walk several hundred meters before you see the Iron-Age fort surrounded by its defensive pointed stones known as *chevaux de frise*. The term *chevaux de frise* is derived from a military expression used to describe how Dutch Frisians used spikes to impede attackers. Ireland has three other such forts, of which the two most impressive are found on the Aran Islands.

When you leave the Burren head directly for the coast and follow it east (N67) to **Kinvara**, a pretty village with boats bobbing in the harbor and small rocky islands separating it from the expanse of Galway Bay. On the outskirts of the village, the restored **Dunguaire Castle** has a craft shop and on summer evenings hosts medieval banquets. (Open Easter-Sep, tel: 091 37108.)

From the castle car park, turn towards the village and immediately take a left-hand turn (opposite the castle entrance) for the 5-kilometer drive to **Ardrahan** where you turn right on the N18, and after 6 kilometers left for the 2-kilometer drive to **Thoor Ballylee**. William Butler Yeats bought this 13th-century tower house and cottage in 1917, and it was his summer home for 11 years. The cozy, thatched cottage is now a book shop and the adjacent tea room with its three-legged bog chairs and welcoming fire provides an excellent excuse to linger over tea and scones or enjoy lunch. An audio-visual presentation tells of Yeats' artistic and political achievements. Two floors of the tower are sparsely furnished as they were in his occupancy. By pressing a green button on each room's wall you receive information and hear excerpts of his poetry. (Open May-Sep, tel: 091 31436.) Leaving Thoor Ballylee, retrace your steps to the N18 for a 24-kilometer drive to Galway.

SIDE TRIP TO THE ARAN ISLANDS

*If you are planning to visit the **Aran Islands**, take the coastal route through Spiddal to **Rossaveel** where two ferry companies operate a shuttle service to **Kilronan** on **Inishmore**, the largest of the three Aran Islands. (Aran Ferries, tel: 091 68903, Island Ferries tel: 091 61767.) Until a decade or so ago, time had stood still here and the way of life and the culture of the islanders had changed little. Now their traditional dress comes out only for TV cameras and special occasions, and their traditional way of life has been replaced by a more profitable one—tourism. In the summertime more than double the population of the islands arrives on Inishmore as day-trippers. On arrival, visit the Tourist Information Centre by the harbor to discuss the appropriate cost of horse and trap, bicycle (there are plenty of shops where you can rent bikes), and minibus transportation. The barren landscape is closely related to that of the Burren: sheer cliffs plunge into the pounding Atlantic Ocean along the southern coast while the north coast flattens out with shallow, rock-ringed sandy beaches. You will have no difficulty obtaining transportation to **Dún Aengus** (about 8 kilometers from the harbor), the best known of the island's stone forts, believed to date from the early Celtic period some 2 to 3,000 years ago. It has sheer cliffs at its back and is surrounded by pointed boulders designed to twist ankles and skin shins. Despite the hordes of visitors scrambling over its walls and stones, it is remarkably well preserved. With four stone forts, stone hut remains, high crosses, and ruined churches to examine, the archaeologically-minded could spend many days with detailed map in hand exploring the islands.*

Those who are not island-bound should follow signs for Clifden (N59) around Galway. Leaving the town behind, the road is straight and well paved, but a tad bouncy if you try to go too fast. Accommodation signs for nearby Oughterard alert you to watch for a right-hand turn to **Aughnanure Castle**. Approaching the castle, you may be greeted, as we were, by a friendly family of goats snoozing on the wooden footbridge before the castle gates. Aughnanure Castle was the stronghold of the ferocious O'Flahertys who launched attacks on Galway town until their castle was destroyed by English forces in

Clifden

1572. The clan regained their castle for a period of time until wars with Cromwell and William of Orange saw them expelled again. (Open Jun-Sep, tel: 091 82214.) Nearby **Oughterard** is a pleasant, bustling town ("the gateway to Connemara") whose main street has several attractive shops. A stay here affords the opportunity for fishing and exploring the island-dotted Lough Corrib by boat.

Beyond Oughterard you plunge into Connemara past the **Twelve Bens** mountains which dominate the wild, almost treeless landscape of bogs, lakes, and rivers, a landscape that is ever being changed by the dashing clouds that rush in from the Atlantic. Apart from the occasional craft shop, there are no houses until you reach **Clifden** on the Atlantic coast (N59, 80 kilometers). Clifden is the major market town of Connemara and the home of the annual Connemara Pony Show (third week in August). The town presents a gay face with shopfronts painted in bright hues of red, blue, yellow, and green. Craft and tourist shops alternate with the butchers, the hardware store, pubs, and restaurants.

SIDE TRIP TO ROUNDSTONE

*To the south of Clifden the road has more views of sea than land as little boats bob in rocky inlets and cottages gaze westward across tiny islands. The road passes the marshy area where Alcock and Brown crash-landed after the first trans-Atlantic flight in 1919 (commemorated by a monument about 500 meters from the main road). Via **Ballinaboy**, **Ballyconneely**, and **Roundstone,** the sweeping seascapes that this route presents are so compelling that it is difficult to concentrate on the driving.*

SIDE TRIP TO INISHBOFIN ISLAND

*If the weather is fine, a delightful day trip can be taken to **Inishbofin Island**. The Inishbofin boat leaves from Cleggan pier at 11:30 am, returning at 5:00 pm (the crossing takes less than an hour). Be at **Cleggan** pier half an hour before sailing time and buy your ticket at the Pier Bar. Sailings depend on weather conditions so it's best to phone ahead at (095) 44261 to verify departure times. The boat sails into the sheltered harbor presided over by the remains of a Cromwellian castle, and you wade ashore at a cluster of houses that make up the island's main settlement. Many islanders have left in search of greener pastures and their cottages have fallen into disrepair, but those who remain eke out a hard living from the land and the sea. As you walk down lanes edged with wild fuschias and brightly-colored wildflowers, whitewashed farmhouses appear and you see fields dotted with handmade haystacks. (Regrettably, the odd long-abandoned rusting car spoils the scene.) At the far side of the island a row of cottages fronts the beach, one of them housing a welcoming little cafe where you can have a lunch or tea before walking back to the harbor to take the evening boat back to Cleggan.*

Doo Lough

Clifden stands just outside the **Connemara National Park** which covers 5,000 acres of mountain, heath, and bog—there are no pretty gardens or verdant woodlands. The video in the visitors' center gives a beautiful introduction to the park which has wonderful hiking trails. If you want to tackle the smaller paths leading into the Twelve Bens mountains, consider joining one of the guided walks that begin at the visitors' center (four of the Twelve Bens, including Benbaum, the highest are found in the park). Two signposted nature trails start at the visitors' center: one leads you through Ellis Wood while the other takes you into rougher terrain. (Open May-Sept.)

Leaving Clifden to the north, the N59 passes the much-photographed **Kylemore Abbey**. Originally built by a wealthy Englishman in the 19th century, this grand home, surrounded by greenery and fronting a lake, passed into the hands of Benedictine nuns who have a school here. There's ample parking and a large restaurant and gift shop. You can walk beside the lake to the abbey where in summer the library is open to visitors. In the grounds you can visit the resored Gothic chapel with its pretty sandstone interior and different colored marble pillars. (Open Apr-Dec, tel: 095 41113.)

Delphi

Follow the shore of **Killary Harbor**, the longest and certainly the most picturesque fjord in Ireland, to **Leenane**, a little village nestled at the head of the inlet. Continue along the shoreline and take the first turn to the left, signposted as a scenic route to Westport via Louisburgh. This interesting side road gently winds you along the sea lough to **Delphi**, an area of pools and loughs amongst some of the highest and wildest mountains in the west. Acres of woodlands offer shelter and there is not a bungalow in sight. The Marquis of Sligo built a lodge here in 1840 and called it "Delphi" because it reminded him of Delphi in Greece. After falling into dereliction, the house and estate were bought by Peter and Jane Mantle who welcome guests to their restored home (see listing under Leenane).

Leaving Delphi, the isolated mountain road takes you along the shore of **Doo Lough** at the foot of **Mweelrea Mountain** and on through wild, remote scenery to **Louisburgh**, where, turning towards Westport, the summit of the conical-shaped **Croagh Patrick** (Ireland's most famous mountain) comes into view. Swirling mists substantiate its mystical place in Irish history. It was after St Patrick spent the 40 days of Lent atop its rocky summit in 441AD that the mountain became sacred to the Christian god. Every year thousands of penitential pilgrims begin their climb to the oratory at the summit at dawn on the last Sunday in July, several going barefoot up the stony track. The ritual involves stopping at three stations and reciting prayers. No climbing skills are needed as it's a well-worn path to the top and on a clear day a walk to the summit affords a panoramic view across Clew Bay to Achill Island.

Nearby **Westport** lies on the shore of Clew Bay and is unique amongst Irish towns because it was built following a pre-designed plan. The architect walled the river and lined the riverside malls with lime trees and austere Georgian homes, forming a most delightful thoroughfare. There's a buzz to the town and on a sunny day you can enjoy a drink at the tables and chairs outside Geraghtey's Bar and Grand Central, on the Octagon (the heart of the town with a granite pillar in the center of the square).

At **Clew Bay Heritage Centre** on Westport Quay, postcards and old photographs show the town as it was at the turn of the century. There is also a genealogical research center and a display on the maritime traditions of Westport. (Open all year, tel: 098 26852.)

From Westport the most direct route to Sligo is by way of the broad, well-paved, fast N60, N5, and N17. However, if the weather is clear and bright, it is a delightful drive from Westport to Sligo via Newport, Achill island, Crossmolina, and Ballina.

Achill Island is Ireland's largest offshore island. Traditionally the Achill islanders traveled to Scotland as migrant farmworkers during the summer, but now what population has not been enticed away by emigration remains to garner a meager living from a harsh land. This was the home of the infamous British Captain Boycott who gave his name to the English language when tenants "boycotted" him for his excessive rents during the potato famine. Today this island holds the allure that belongs to wild and lonely places: in sunshine it is glorious, but in torrential rain it is a grim and depressing place.

Croagh Patrick

On the island take the first turn to your left, signposted for the windswept **Atlantic Drive,** where you drive along the tops of rugged cliffs carved by the pounding Atlantic Ocean far below. The "drive" ends at **Knockmore** where scattered houses shelter from the biting winds.

Returning to Mulrany, turn north on the N59 for the 32-kilometer drive across boglands, where vast quantities of turf are harvested by mechanical means, to **Bangor** and on to **Crossmolina, Ballina,** and Sligo. The many sightseeing opportunities in the Sligo area are outlined in the following itinerary.

The West

SIDE TRIP TO CÉIDE FIELDS

*From Ballina you can detour north 20 kilometers to Ballycastle and drive another 8 kilometers east to the great cliffs of **Downpatrick Head** where the Stone-Age settlements at **Céide Fields** (pronounced kay-jeh) are being excavated. Under the peat has been unearthed the most extensive Stone-Age settlement in the world, its walls are older than the pyramids, a vast site which once supported a community of over 10,000 people. Wander round a portion of the archaeological dig and enjoy an audio visual presentation and a cup of tea in the pyramid-shaped visitors' center. (Open May-Oct, tel: 096 43325.) The surrounding cliffs are amongst the most magnificent you will see in Ireland. Retrace your steps to Ballycastle and take the R314 through **Killale** (a workaday village whose skyline is punctuated by an ancient round tower) to **Ballina** where you turn left for **Sligo**.*

From the Sligo area you can go into Northern Ireland, continue north on the following itinerary, or return south. If you travel south, consider visiting either **Ballintubber Abbey**, a beautifully restored church dating back to 1216, or the village of **Knock**. A religious apparition seen on the gable of the village church in 1879 and some hearty promotion has led to the development of Knock as a religious pilgrimage site and a tourist venue. A giant basilica stands next to the little church, a large complex of religious souvenir shops is across the road, and nearby Knock airport has a runway capable of providing landing facilities for large jets. Surrounded as it is by narrow country lanes, this sophisticated complex seems very out of place in rural Ireland.

The West

The North

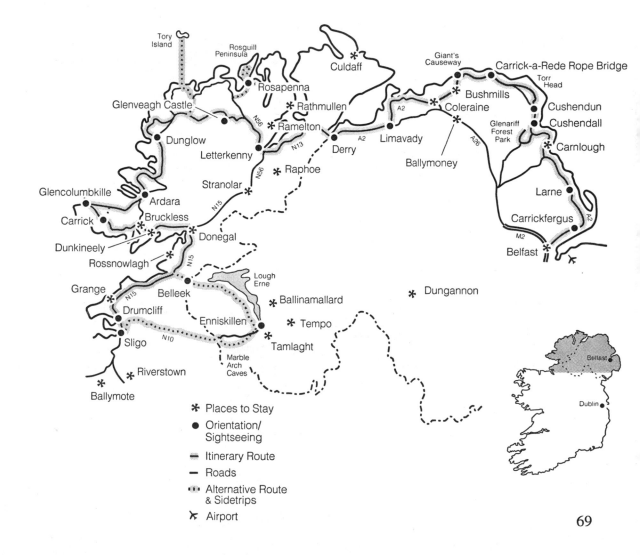

Tory Island

Rosguill Peninsula

Culdaff

Giant's Causeway

Carrick-a-Rede Rope Bridge

Rosapenna

Torr Head

Bushmills

Cushendun

* Rathmullen

Coleraine

Cushendall

Glenveagh Castle

A2

Glenariff Forest Park

* Ramelton

Dunglow

A2

Carnlough

N56

Letterkenny

Derry

Limavady

A26

Ballymoney

N13

Larne

Stranolar

* Raphoe

N56

Carrickfergus

Glencolumbkille

Ardara

N15

Bruckless

Donegal

M2

Belfast

Carrick

Dunkineely

Rossnowlagh

N15

Lough Erne

Grange

Belleek

* Ballinamallard

* Dungannon

Drumcliff

Enniskillen

* Tempo

N10

Tamlaght

Sligo

Marble Arch Caves

* Riverstown

Ballymote

* Places to Stay

● Orientation/ Sightseeing

▬ Itinerary Route

▬ Roads

▪▪▪ Alternative Route & Sidetrips

✈ Airport

Belfast

Dublin

69

The North

The northernmost reaches of Ireland hold special appeal. Herein lies the countryside that inspired the moving poetry of William Butler Yeats. Beyond Donegal narrow roads twist and turn around the wild, rugged coastline of County Donegal where villagers weave their tweeds and Irish is often the spoken language and that written on the signposts. The Folk Village Museum at Glencolumbkille, with its authentically-furnished, thatch-topped cottages, demonstrates the harsh living conditions of the far north. Crossing into Northern Ireland, the honeycomb columns of the Giant's Causeway signpost the Antrim coast full of cliffs, lush, green headlands, and beautiful views. As you cross the border you are scrutinized at a military border crossing and you may see the occasional army patrol on the road, but more than likely all you will see is glorious countryside.

Dunluce Castle

RECOMMENDED PACING: Two or three nights around Sligo and Donegal, a night near Glenveagh National Park (to permit a leisurely visit), and two nights along the Antrim coast will afford you time to explore this lovely area.

The county and town of **Sligo** are ever mindful of William Butler Yeats, and the whole area is promoted as being Yeats country. If you are an ardent admirer of the poet, you will want to visit the **County Museum** which has a special section about his poetry and writing. Base yourself near the town for several days—Ballymote and Riverstown are our accommodation choices in the *Places to Stay* section. The countryside is very pretty and there is enough sightseeing to keep you busy for a week.

SIDE TRIP TO CARROWMORE AND CARROWKEEL

Seven kilometers to the southwest of Sligo town, sitting in fields on either side of a narrow country lane, are the megalithic tombs of **Carrowmore**. *Wander amongst the cows and explore the little stone circles and larger dolmens reputed to be the largest Bronze-Age cemetery in Europe. Farther inland (take the Boyle road (N4) 30 kilometers south of Sligo to Castlebaldwin where you turn right following signposts for Carrowkeel. At the end of a mountain track you come to* **Carrowkeel**, *a 4,000-year-old passage tomb cemetery. There are thirteen cairns which cover passage tombs while the fourteenth is a long cairn. One of the tombs can be entered (backwards) and it is claimed that, on the summer solstice, the setting sun lights up the main chamber.*

SIDE TRIP 'ROUND LOUGH GILL

A half-day sightseeing trip from Sligo can be taken by driving around Lough Gill, visiting Parke's Castle and enjoying a meal at Markree Castle. Leave Sligo to the north and follow signposts for Enniskillen, Lough Derg, and Dromohair which bring you to the northerly shore of **Lough Gill**. *Glimpses of the lough through the trees give way to stunning lough views as the road hugs the shore and arrives at* **Parke's Castle**, *a fortified manor house whose ramparts and cottages (tea rooms) have been restored. (Open Easter-Oct, tel: 071 64149.) In summer you can take a boat trip on the lake which* *takes you around* **Inishfree Island***. Leaving the castle, follow the lough into* **Dromohair** *where you pick up the Sligo road. After 5 kilometers, when the road divides, take a single track lane to the right which leads you down to the lakeside where John O'Connel's rowboat is tied to the pier. He lives by the lake and is sometimes available to row you to Inishfree Island. Returning to the main road, it's a short drive to* **Collonney** *where you can partake of lunch or afternoon tea at* **Markree Castle***.*

Leaving Sligo, travel north along the N15 to **Drumcliff Churchyard**, which has to be the most visited graveyard in Ireland—William Butler Yeats is buried here under the epitaph he composed, "Cast a cold eye on life, on death. Horseman pass by!" In the background is the imposing **Benbulben Mountain**. Beyond the village a left turn leads to **Lissadell,** home of the Gore-Booth sisters with whom Yeats was friendly. The 1830's Greek-Revival-style house is full of curiosities and quite a sight to behold, but in need of an injection of capital to prevent its decay. The room where Yeats stayed is over the porch. While the sisters belonged to the landed gentry, Eva went on to become a poet and Constance, a suffragette commander in the 1916 uprising and a minister of labor in the first Irish government. Sir Henry Gore-Booth went off with his butler to explore the Antarctic in the 1880s. (Open intermittently, usually Jun-Sep, closed Sun, tel: 071 63150.)

Leaving Lissadell continue north on the N15 for the 60-kilometer drive to Donegal or follow a more circuitous route through Northern Ireland.

ALTERNATIVE ROUTE TO DONEGAL

*From Drumcliff churchyard, return towards Sligo and at **Rathcormack** turn left through the village of **Drum** to join the N16 as it travels east towards **Enniskillen**. After checking with the guard at the border post, take the first turn to your right and follow signposts to **Marble Arch Caves**. This extensive network of limestone chambers (billed as "over 300 million years of history") is most impressive. The tour includes an underground boat journey, walks through large illuminated chambers, galleries hung with remarkable stalactites, and a "Moses Walk" along a man-made passage through a lake where your feet are at the bottom of the pool and your head is at the same level as the water. Remember to dress warmly and take a sweater. It is best to telephone in advance because if there has been a lot of rain, the caves are closed. (Open Mar-Oct, tel: 01365 348855.)*

*Leaving the hilltop cave complex, follow signposts for Enniskillen for 7 kilometers to **Florence Court**, an 18th-century mansion that was once the home of the Earls of Enniskillen. The opulent mansion is elegantly furnished and famous for the impressive Rococo plasterwork on the ceilings. (Open Apr-Oct, tel: 01365 348349.) Leaving Florence Court do not go into Enniskillen, but turn left onto the A46, following the scenic southern shore of **Lough Erne** for the 38- kilometer drive to Belleek.*

***Belleek** on the far north shore of the lough is famous for its ornate, creamy pottery: porcelain festooned with shamrocks or delicate, spaghetti-like strands woven into trellis-like plates. You can tour the visitors' center and then browse at the factory shop. (Open May-Sep.) Crossing back into the Republic, head for **Ballyshannon** and follow the wide N15 north for 23 kilometers to Donegal.*

Glencolumbkille

Donegal is a busy, bustling place, laid out around a diamond-shaped area surrounded by shops. **Magees** sells a variety of tweed items and the **Four Masters Bookshop** is a handy place to stock up on reading material. The ruins of **Donegal Castle** (not open to the public), built in the 16th century by Hugh O'Donell, stand beside the Diamond.

The N56 heads west, hugging the coast, through **Dunkineely** and **Bruckless** (both of which offer excellent places to stay at Castle Murray House and Bruckless House) to **Killybegs**, Ireland's major fishing port. Large trawlers from all over the world have replaced family fishing boats in the harbor of this most enjoyable working town. As you move west from Killybegs, the roads become more difficult, the landscape more rugged, and the signposts less frequent, and to complicate things, are often written in Irish (Irish names are referenced in parentheses).

If the weather is fine, you can enjoy some spectacular scenery by following the brown signs that indicate a coastal route from **Kilcar** to **Carrick** (An Charraig) where you turn left (in the center of the village opposite the pub) for **Telin** (Teilean) and follow the brown signs for **Bunglar** and The Cliffs. As the narrow road winds up and down and around the rocky, rolling landscape you see several examples of traditional Irish cottages with small thatched pony-cart barns huddled next to them. The road narrows to a single track and takes you along the very edge of the headlands to a viewpoint that overlooks the spot where the **Slieve League Cliffs** plummet into the sea. Walkers will love the magnificent walks along the headlands. This is not a trip to be taken in inclement weather.

Retrace your steps to Carrick and turn left towards **Glencolumbkille** (Gleann Cholaim Cille). The road enters the Owenwee Valley where you climb before descending into the glen. Drive through the scattered village to **Glencolumbkille Folk Village Museum** at the water's edge. Glencolumbkille is a very special place that gives an appreciation of the survival of a people who endured hardship, famine, and debilitating emigration. By the 1960s, emigration was threatening to turn Glencolumbkille into a ghost town. In an effort to try to create some jobs, the parish priest, Father McDyer, formed a cooperative of the remaining local residents to develop a tourist industry by building a folk museum and holiday homes and by encouraging local crafts. Tucked against a rocky hillside, the cottages that comprise the folk museum are grouped to form a traditional tiny village, or "clachan." Each cottage is a replica of those lived in by local people in each of three successive centuries. The thick, thatched roofs are tied down with heavy rope and anchored with stones, securing them from the harsh Atlantic winds. Inside, the little homes are furnished with period furniture and utensils. Friendly locals guide you through the houses and give you snippets of local history. A handicraft shop sells Irish cottage crafts and the adjacent tea room serves oven-fresh scones and piping hot tea on lovely Irish pottery. (Open Apr-Oct, tel: 073 30017.)

Leaving Glencolumbkille, the narrow road climbs and dips through seemingly uninhabited, rugged countryside where the views are often obscured by swirling mists as you climb the Glengesh Pass before dropping down into **Ardara**.

The road skirts the coast and brings you to the twin fishing villages of **Portnoo** and **Nairn,** set amongst isolated beaches that truly have an "end-of-the-earth" quality about them. A short drive brings you to **Maas** whence you travel an extremely twisty road to the Gweebarra bridge which brings you to **Lettermacaward** (Leitir Mhic An Bhaird) and on to **Dunglow** (An Globhan Liath). Nearby in **Burtonport** (Ailt An Chorain) more salmon and lobster are landed than at any other port. From here you drive north to **Kincasslagh** and then it's on to **Annagary**, both tiny little communities that pride themselves on speaking the Irish language. A combination of wild, untamed scenery, villages that seem untouched by the 20th century, and narrow, curving roads in general disrepair gives the feeling that the passage of time stopped many years ago in this isolated corner of Ireland.

Rejoin the N56 just south of **Gweedore** (Gaoth Dobhair) and follow it for a short distance as it swings inland paralleling a sea loch. As the main road swings to the right, continue straight up the mountain, following a narrow, winding road that brings you across peat bogs and purple, heather-covered moorlands inhabited only by sheep to **Glenveagh National Park**, Ireland's largest, most natural, and most beautiful park. At its center lies a sheltered glen with a lake and mighty castle. The **Glenveagh Visitors Centre** is well signposted and well disguised, being sunk into the ground with its roof camouflaged by peat and heather. There are displays, an audio-visual program, and a cafe (there's another at the castle) and it is here that you leave your car to take the mini bus around the lake to **Glenveagh Castle** and its gardens. The heather and rose gardens, the rhododendrons, the laurels and pines, busts, and statues are all lovingly maintained, but the walled kitchen garden is especially memorable, with its profusion of flowers and tidy rows of vegetables divided by narrow, grass walkways. Surrounding this oasis of cultivated beauty are thousands of acres of wild countryside where the largest herd of red deer in Ireland roam. Glenveagh Castle was built in 1870 by John Adair, using his American wife's money, in a fanciful Gothic design that was popular in the later part of the century. The rooms have been beautifully restored and for a small entrance fee you can tour the house (arrive by 2:00 pm if you're traveling in July and August). The Glenveagh estate was sold to the nation by the castle's second owner, Henry McIlhenny, who is largely responsible for the design of the gardens. (Open Apr-Oct, tel: 074 37072.)

Leaving the national park, turn right across the desolate boglands and heather-clad hills—your destination is **Glebe House and Gallery** (6 kilometers away) near the village of **Churchhill**. Derek Hill gave his home, Glebe House, and his art collection to the state which remodeled the outbuildings to display his fine collection of paintings. Among the 300 paintings are works by Picasso, Bonnard, Yeats, Annigoni, and Pasmore. The decoration in the house includes William Morris papers and textiles, Victoriana, Donegal Folk Art, and Japanese and Islamic Art. There is a tea room in the courtyard. (Open May-Sep, closed Fri, tel: 074 37071.)

SIDE TRIP TO THE ROSGUILL PENINSULA AND TORY ISLAND

*If you would like to experience more Donegal coastal landscape, you can do no better than tour the **Rosguill Peninsula** whose 25-kilometer Atlantic drive traces a wild coastal drive from **Rosapenna** through **Downies** and **Doagh** to **Tranarossan Bay** and back to Rosapenna. The road goes up and down, most of the time high above the ocean, then sweeps down to white, sandy beaches.*

*If you follow the coastal road west through **Gortahawk** you come to **Meenlaragh** where you take the ferry to **Tory Island**, a windswept island where the inhabitants eke out a hard life farming and fishing. Sailing times of the ferry boat depend on the weather. If you want to visit the island, contact the Post Office in Meenlaragh.*

Giant's Causeway

From Glebe gallery it is a 16-kilometer drive to **Letterkenny**. From the town, your route into Northern Ireland is well signposted to **Derry,** with stops at customs and the army checkpoint—the only reminders that you are crossing from Eire to Ulster. The N13 becomes the A2 as you cross the border and pound sterling becomes the currency. Skirt Derry city on the **Foyle Bridge,** then follow the A2 to **Limavady** and the A37 for 21 kilometers to **Coleraine.**

Bushmills and the Giant's Causeway are well signposted from the outskirts of Coleraine. (One of the delights of traveling in Northern Ireland is that the roads are well paved and the signposting frequent and accurate.) **Bushmills** is famous for its whiskey—a whiskey spelled with an "e"—of which Special Old Black Bush is the best. A tour of the factory demonstrates how they turn barley and water into whiskey and rewards you with a sample of the classic drink to fortify you for your visit to the nearby Giant's Causeway. (Open weekdays, tel: 012657 31521.)

In the last century the **Giant's Causeway** was thought to be one of the wonders of the world. Formed from basaltic rock which cooled and split into regular prismatic shapes, it stepped out to sea to build an irregular honeycomb of columns some 70,000,000 years ago. More romantic than scientific fact is the legend that claims the causeway was built by the Irish giant, Finn MacCool, to get at his rival in Scotland. Do not expect the columns to be tall—for they are not. It is their patterns that make them interesting, not their size.

The first stop on a visit to the Causeway is the **Giant's Causeway Centre** where the facts and legends about the Causeway are well presented in an audio-visual theater. (Open all year, tel: 012657 31855.) A mini bus takes you to the head of the causeway where you follow the path past formations called "Honeycomb," "Wishing Well," "Giant's Granny," "King and his Nobles," "Port na Spaniagh" (where gold and silver treasure from the Spanish Armada ship *Girona* was found in 1967), and "Lovers' Leap" and up the wooden staircase to the headlands where you walk back to the visitors' center along the clifftops. (It's a 5-kilometer walk and you can truly say you have seen the causeway if you complete the circuit.)

Leaving the Causeway, turn right along the coast to visit the ruins of the nearby **Dunluce Castle**, a romantic ruin clinging to a wave-lashed cliff with a great cave right underneath. This was the main fort of the Irish MacDonnells, chiefs of Antrim, and fell into the ruin after the kitchen (and cooks!) fell into the sea during a storm. (Open Apr-Sep, tel: 012657 235000.)

Retrace your route down the B146, and at the Causeway gates turn left along the coast road. Watch carefully for a small plaque at the side of the road pointing out the very meager ruins of **Dunseverick Castle**. Dunseverick was at the northernmost end of the Celtic road where the Celts crossed to and from Scotland.

Shortly after joining the A2, turn left for **Port Bradon**. The road winds down to the sea where a hamlet of gaily-painted houses and a church nestle around a sheltered harbor. As

Carrick-a-Rede Rope Bridge

you stand in front of the smallest church in Ireland, the long, sandy beaches of **Whitepark Bay** stretch before you.

Farther along the coast a narrow road winds down to the very picturesque **Ballintoy Harbour,** a sheltered haven for boats surrounded by small, jagged, rocky islands. At the first road bend after leaving Ballintoy village, turn sharp left for the **Carrick-a-Rede Rope Bridge.** This is one of the famous things to do in Ireland: walk high above the sea across a narrow, swinging bridge of planks and ropes that joins a precipitous cliff to a rocky island. Hardy fishermen whose cottages and nets nestle in a sheltered cleft on the island and whose fragile wooden boats bob in the ocean below still use the bridge. (Open May-Sep, tel: 012657 31159.)

Life in the nearby holiday town of **Ballycastle** centers around the beach, fishing, and golf. Cross the river and turn onto the A2 to **Ballyvoy**. If the weather is clear, turn left for the scenic drive to Cushendun round **Torr Head**. The narrow road, barely wide enough for two cars to pass, switchbacks across the headlands and corkscrews down the cliffside, offering spectacular views of the rugged coastline and the distant Mull of Kintyre in Scotland.

Nestling by the seashore, the pretty village of **Cushendun** has a National Trust Shop, an excellent place to buy high quality souvenirs. When you leave Cushendun, the landscape softens and the road, thankfully, returns to a more manageable width. You are now entering the **Glens of Antrim** where lush, green fields and a succession of beautiful views present themselves. At **Cushendall** you can detour into **Glenariff Forest Park**, the queen of the glens with a series of waterfalls plunging down a gorge traversed by a scenic path crossing rustic bridges. Thackeray described this glen as "Switzerland in miniature." (Open all year, tel: 012667 58232.)

After your return to the coast road, **Carnlough**, a pretty seaside and fishing town, soon comes into view, its little white harbor full of bobbing boats. The Londonderry Arms was once a coaching inn and now is a very pleasant family hotel (see listing).

Nearby **Glenarm** is the oldest of the coastal villages, dating back to the time of King John. The pseudo-Gothic castle is the home of the Earl of Antrim, part of whose demesne, **Glenarm Forest**, climbs up from the glen and is open to the public. (Open all year.)

Limestone cliffs present themselves as you approach **Larne**, a sizable seaport whose Viking origins are lost amongst more modern commercial developments. Wend your way through this busy port town, following the A2 to **Whitehead**. Nearby **Carrickfergus** is the oldest town in Northern Ireland. **Carrickfergus Castle** is a sturdy, Norman castle overlooking the boat-filled harbor. The castle was built as a stronghold in 1178 by John de Courcy after his invasion of Ulster, then taken by King John after a siege in 1210, fell to the Scots in 1316, and was captured by the French in 1760. Life-size models and a film recreate the castle's turbulent past. (Open all year, tel: 01960 351273.)

Leaving Carrickfergus a 12-kilometer drive along the A2 and M2/M1 whisks you through, or into, **Belfast**, where the A1 will take you south through **Newry** and into the Republic. Or, if you are staying near the Antrim coast for several days of leisurely sightseeing, take the M2 to the A26 which quickly returns you to your base.

Carrickfergus Castle

Places to Stay

This noble house with ornate Gothic facades stands amidst a vast estate separated from the charming village of Adare by a high stone wall and iron gates. It was rescued from decline by Tom Kane, a third-generation Galway emigrant, and his wife Judy and transformed into a luxury resort. Built as the elaborate home of the Earls of Dunraven, the house was constructed on a massive scale with a two-story-high paneled reception, over 50 hand-carved fireplaces, and an enormous, ornate gallery based on the Hall of Mirrors in Versailles. In the original manor, bedrooms and suites are baronial in size with elaborately carved marble fireplaces, king-sized beds, and seating arrangements. Bathrooms have marble floors and walls, huge tubs, and generous-sized dressing rooms. Bedrooms in the new wing are less opulent. All has been immaculately restored to reflect a luxurious, 19th-century country-house atmosphere, yet this is a mix of old and modern. In the vast grounds are the remains of a Franciscan priory built in 1464, the square keep of a feudal castle, a pets' graveyard, and a championship golf course designed by Robert Trent Jones, Sr. There is also a luxurious indoor swimming pool, gymnasium, sauna, snooker room and tack-room bar complete with Irish music. Riding with the Dunraven hunt is an attraction, as are clay pigeon shooting and fishing in the River Maigue. *Directions:* Adare Manor is in the village of Adare, a 45-minute drive from Shannon airport.

ADARE MANOR
Owners: Judy and Tom Kane
Adare
Co Limerick
tel: (061) 396566, fax: (061) 396124
63 ensuite rooms
Double from £220
Open all year
Credit cards: all major
Luxury resort

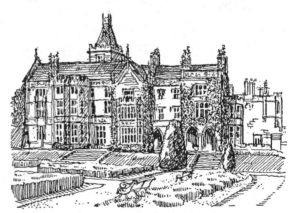

The Dunraven Arms stands on the broad main street of this storybook village, its flower-filled garden adding to the picturesque scene. With its uniformed staff and formal restaurant it has more the feel of a hunting lodge than a hostelry. The hotel is smartly decorated and attractive antique furniture adds to the old-world feeling. The large informal bar is the gathering place for locals and residents alike, but if you want a few quiet moments, there is a snug residents' lounge with chintz-covered chairs gathered round a log fire (the inn is a popular venue for weddings). To guarantee a quiet night's sleep, request a room in the new wing that extends behind the inn into the peaceful garden. As well as being most attractively decorated, these new rooms enjoy immaculate modern bathrooms. The dining room has quite a reputation for its food—a laden dessert cart sits center stage and waiters hover attentively. If more informal dining is to your taste, visit the hotel's cozy restaurant, The Inn Between, in a quaint, thatched cottage across the street. The hotel specializes in making golfing, equestrian, and fishing arrangements for guests. A 12½% service charge is added to your bill. *Directions:* Adare is on the N21, 40 kilometers from Shannon airport, which makes it an ideal first or last stop in Ireland if you are going to or coming from the southwest.

DUNRAVEN ARMS
Managers: Bryan and Louis Murphy
Adare
Co Limerick
tel: (061) 396633, fax: (061) 396541
45 ensuite rooms
Double from £122
Open all year
Credit cards: all major
Inn

Adare is such a lovely village with its wide main street and quaint, thatched cottages that while I have two other listings here, I searched to find the very best bed and breakfast accommodation and was delighted when I arrived at Margaret and John Shovlin's home, Sandfield House. John is the food and beverage manager at the Dunraven Arms and Margaret has opened up their redbrick home as a bed and breakfast. Margaret offers no meals except breakfast, but restaurants to suit every taste and budget are just a few minutes' drive away in the village. Margaret often finds herself fixing a welcoming pot of tea for exhausted guests who arrive direct from their transatlantic flights from nearby Shannon airport. The lounge provides a quiet place to sit and there is lots of information on the village and nearby attractions. Upstairs are three modern, comfortable bedrooms each with bathrooms neatly tucked into the corner. Plans are going ahead to add an additional larger bedroom with roomy bathroom for the summer of 1995. *Directions:* From Shannon airport take the N18 to Limerick and the N20 to the N21 (Killarney road) to Adare. Turn left at the beginning of the wall at the grey stone building on the N21 and continue for 3 kilometers, the house is on your right.

SANDFIELD HOUSE
Owners: Margaret and John Shovlin
Castleroberts
Adare
Co Limerick
tel: (061) 396119
4 ensuite rooms
From £15 per person B&B
Open all year
Credit cards: EC, MC, VS
B&B

Set about halfway between Dublin and Rosslare Harbor, Plattenstown House is an ideal base for exploring County Wicklow, "The Garden of Ireland," with its heather-clad hills, pretty farmland, sandy beaches, and outstanding houses and gardens. Set in its own attractive gardens and surrounded by peaceful countryside, Plattenstown House was built in 1853. When their children had grown, Margaret found the house too large for herself and her husband and so decided to take guests. She is a warm, hospitable person who puts a lot of effort into pleasing her visitors. While there are several restaurants in Arklow, Margaret finds that guests often want to stay in after a day sightseeing and she is happy to cook them dinner or a light supper (she makes the most delicious soups) with notice as late as early afternoon. Guests have a drawing room and a snug television room. Upstairs the most spacious bedroom, Anna Livia, has a most unusual set of curvaceous, light-wood furniture hand-crafted in the 1930s. Furniture by the same cabinetmaker graces the dining room while the remainder of the house is in a more traditional, old-fashioned vein. Gordon used to be a dairy farmer, but now he raises calves and is happy to take guests across the garden and introduce them to his "mums" and their gentle offspring. *Directions:* Leave the N11 at the roundabout at the top of Arklow town, take the Coolgreaney road for 4 kilometers and the house is on your left.

PLATTENSTOWN HOUSE   **NEW**
Owners: Margaret and Gordon McDowell
Coolgreaney Road
Arklow
Co Wicklow
tel: (0402) 32582
4 ensuite rooms
From £18 per person B&B
Open March to November
Credit cards: EC, MC, VS
Farmhouse B&B

Ashley House is a large modern bungalow on a quiet country lane just to the north of Ballina town, built on the May River—famous for salmon fishing. Carmel Murray, its owner, is a keen gardener and in summer her garden is a profusion of colorful flowers and heathers. The neat-as-a-new-pin look of the garden is extended to the home's pristine interior with its prettily papered walls and matching floral drapes. Carmel welcomes her guests with tea and cakes and has compiled a scrapbook of all the things there are to do in the area. Breakfast is the only meal served; for dinner, guests often go to Brogans bar and restaurant in town. Bedrooms come with one, two, and three beds and while each is different in its decor, they are most attractive, with frilly muslin sheers and flowered drapes, wallpaper and bedspreads. In summer there is often traditional Irish music and set-dancing locally on Thursdays (Carmel is an enthusiastic set-dancer). Ballina is between two very popular sightseeing venues, Céide Fields and Foxford Woolen Mills. High atop a cliff near Ballycastle, the Stone-Age settlement at Céide Fields has been excavated and a visitors center shows you how this outpost supported people. Foxford Woolen Mills has been restored and you can see craftspeople produce tweeds, rugs and blankets and enjoy an audio-visual showing life at Foxford. *Directions:* From Ballina take the N59 in the direction of Belmullet for a kilometer and turn right at the signpost.

ASHLEY HOUSE **NEW**
Owners: Carmel and Michael Murray
Ardoughan
Ballina
Co Mayo
tel: (096) 22799
5 rooms, 3 ensuite
From £14 per person B&B
Open March to November
Credit cards: EC, MC, VS
B&B

Built in 1760, Whaley Abbey was once the shooting lodge of the playboy, Buck Whiley, whose outrageous exploits are celebrated in the colorful cartoons that hang on the living-room wall. For many years this was Emir's (pronounced Ema's) weekend home where she entertained friends and family: now the only difference is that the house is open year-round and friends are given a bill. While her home is beautifully decorated with great style, Emir takes special pride in her hot-water system that guarantees plentiful hot showers. On cool days there's always a fire ablaze in the cheery living room and guests dine together 'round the large refectory table where the main course is often a traditional roast. Bedrooms come in all sizes, from the spaciousness of Emir's room (all decked out in country pine with a semi-circular tub in the bathroom) to the snug attic room found up a steep flight of narrow stairs. The Conservatory room has the advantage of opening up to a small conservatory with inviting armchairs. Riding stables are a five-minute drive away and Glendalough and the Vale of Avoca are close at hand. *Directions:* From Dublin take the N11 (Wicklow road) to Rathnew where you turn right on the R752 for Rathdrum and Avoca. About 1.5 kilometers beyond Rathdrum turn right for Ballinaclash, and after going over the river, continue straight up the hill and take the first left, following this road until it becomes a track. Whaley Abbey is the first house on your right.

WHALEY ABBEY **NEW**
Owners: Emir and Liam Shanahan
Ballinaclash
Rathdrum
Co Wicklow
tel: (0404) 46529, fax: (0404) 46793
7 ensuite rooms
From £25 per person B&B
Open April to October
Credit cards: all major
Country house

Glebe House, an impressive Georgian rectory standing amidst a flower-filled garden, is home to Tim and Gill Bracken and their two young children. Tim works as a lawyer in Cork and returns home in the evening to a house full of guests. Tim loves to cook and is happy to provide dinner, which is served on the polished mahogany table. Glebe House does not have a wine license so guests are encouraged to bring a bottle of wine to enjoy with their meal. Upstairs, two of the three bedrooms are named for their color theme. The Blue Room, a small romantic double, has a large flowing canopy over the Georgian brass bed, while The Green Room boasts a huge flowery bathroom with an antique hobby-horse tricycle in the corner. The Twin Room contains both a single and a double bed. In the former stables are two very attractive self catering units. Across the Bandon River and round the headland, Kinsale comes into view, its harbor full of tall-masted sail boats and its narrow, winding streets full of slate-hung houses, tempting restaurants, and fine sea views. If peace and quiet are more to your taste, follow the coast road west through peaceful villages and rolling countryside past quiet beaches. *Directions:* Take the N71 from Cork through Innishannon, turn sharp left after the bridge, and Glebe House is the first house on the right before you enter the village.

GLEBE HOUSE
Owners: Gill and Tim Bracken
Ballinadee
Bandon
Kinsale
Co Cork
tel: (021) 778294, fax: (021) 778456
3 ensuite rooms
From £22.50 per person B&B
Open May to November
Credit cards: none
Country house

Jamestown House is in the heart of one of the most popular field sports areas in Ireland and there can be no greater enthusiast for the sporting life than your host, Arthur Stuart. He offers guests a wide variety of sporting opportunities from fishing for brown trout to shooting snipe, woodcock, and wild pheasant. The Stuarts' classic Georgian home is large enough for guests and their young family, and they have made it into a comfortable and unpretentious place to stay. Of the three large bedrooms, I particularly liked the double bedroom that faces the back of the house with its flowery wallpaper, matching drapes and bedspreads, and large bathroom. I found the large metal-box showers in the other two bathrooms rather off-putting. Afternoon tea and biscuits are served in the drawing room, and it is here that guests gather before dinner round the long, polished dining-room table. We have received letters of praise for Arthur who (despite having guests who have returned regularly for fishing and shooting) went out of his way to entertain his non-sporting company. In nearby Enniskillen, Castlecoole, Ireland's finest classical mansion, is open to the public. A few kilometers farther afield is the extensive network of underground chambers that makes up the impressive Marble Arch Caves. *Directions:* From Enniskillen take the A32 towards Irvinestown. Turn right on the B46 to Ballinamallard, go through the village, and continue for just a few kilometers: Jamestown House is signposted on your left.

JAMESTOWN HOUSE
Owners: Helen and Arthur Stuart
Ballinamallard
Co Fermanagh
tel: (0365) 81209
3 ensuite rooms
From £25 per person B&B
Closed Christmas
Credit cards: none
Country house

Set on the shores of Lough Derg, the largest lake on the River Shannon, Gurthalougha House is a delightfully old-fashioned country home run with great enthusiasm by Michael and Bessie Wilkinson. Bessie offers a warm welcome and Michael is a man who loves to cook. It is a winning combination, and between them they run a welcoming place with the minimum amount of regimentation. The house is large and rambling and there is a captivating charm to the place. To my delight, a recent visit saw great improvements in the bedrooms, and while they are not filled with antique furniture, they are very comfortable. Worn carpets and old drapes have been replaced, the walls are freshly painted and new linoleum spruces up the bathrooms. Breakfast is as early or late as you desire and can be taken in bed if you wish. Dinner is wonderful, served entirely by the soft flicker of candlelight. The dinner menu offers choices in all but the soup course. The adjacent lough is an ideal spot for fishermen, and, even if you don't fish, a delightful place to row. Situated just an hour and a half drive from Shannon airport, this is an ideal base for visiting Clonmacnois (the remains of a 6th century monastic city beside the River Shannon), Yeats home (Thoor Ballylee) and Lady Gregory's Coole Park. *Directions:* Gurthalougha House is located 26 kilometers north of Nenagh (N52) between the villages of Terryglass and Ballinderry—the house is signposted in Ballinderry.

GURTHALOUGHA HOUSE
Owners: Bessie and Michael Wilkinson
Ballinderry
Borrisokane
Nenagh
Co Tipperary
tel: (067) 22080, fax: (067) 22154
8 ensuite rooms
Double from £70
Closed February
Credit cards: EC, MC, VS
Country house

Ballydehob is a colorfully painted village set amongst ruggedly beautiful countryside. Fortunately for visitors to this most attractive spot, there is an attractive bed and breakfast, Lynwood, just a short walk from town. Ann is the most welcoming of hostesses and she makes as much effort with her home as she does with her guests—her latest addition to her prettily decorated bedrooms are televisions, hairdryers, and electric blankets. All the guestrooms have tea and coffee makings and compact, ensuite shower rooms. A conservatory overlooks a tennis court that guests are welcome to use. For dinner most visitors go to the Ballydehob Inn or to Annie's Restaurant, because breakfast is the only meal that Ann serves. The road to Mizen Head takes travelers through Schull and past Barley Cove, a flat, sandy beach, to the southwestern tip of Ireland where vertical sandstone cliffs plunge into the sea— the last little bit of Ireland that so many emigrants saw as they sailed for America. The road back along the northern coast of the peninsula is very beautiful. *Directions:* Ballydehob is just off the N71 (Cork to Killarney road). Follow the Schull road through the village and Lynwood is on your right.

LYNWOOD
Owner: Ann Vaughan
Schull Road
Ballydehob
Co Cork
tel: (028) 37124
3 ensuite rooms
From £15 per person B&B
Open April to October
Credit cards: none
B&B

This tall, bright white Victorian house is set amidst lush gardens that rim the shores of Bantry Bay. Although it is worth a stay here just to soak up the spectacular scenery, the house has much to offer. Kathleen O'Sullivan is an energetic hostess, often kept busy behind the scenes seeing that guests are well taken care of and well fed. The sitting room/bar, pretty in soft pinks and blues with light wood furniture, offers plenty of places to sit, and for those in search of peace and quiet there is an old-fashioned parlor/TV room. The spacious bedrooms are individually decorated, those at the front of the house having the advantage of views of Bantry Bay through the trees. The Garden Room, on the ground floor, has been specially equipped for the handicapped. In addition, Kathleen has two very comfortable cottages on the grounds, just the place for families, friends traveling together, or those who prefer self catering. The atmosphere is friendly and informal, which accounts, I am sure, for the large number of guests who return here year after year. Wander off the main roads to explore the Beara Peninsula with its astonishing views of barren, rocky mountains tumbling into the sea. A "must visit" is nearby Garinish Island, a spectacular botanical garden with trees, shrubs, and plants from every part of the world. Also nearby is Bantry House, a grand mansion commanding the loveliest of views of Bantry Bay. *Directions:* Sea View House Hotel is located in Ballylickey on the N71 between Bantry and Glengariff.

SEA VIEW HOUSE HOTEL
Owner: Kathleen O'Sullivan
Ballylickey
Co Cork
tel: (027) 50462, fax: (027) 51555
18 ensuite rooms
Double from £90
Open April to October
Credit cards: all major
Country house hotel

Sir William is the twelfth generation of the Moore family to live at Moore Lodge, an elegant plantation house dating back to 1620, sitting high above the River Bann. Sir William and Lady Gillian welcome guests as they would family friends, encouraging them to make themselves at home in the elegant drawing room or the snug parlor. Conversation often turns to all things fishing, for the River Bann is famous for its salmon fishing (June to September) and coarse fishing. Guests can be kitted out with rods, and Sir William is often willing to take experienced fisherfolk on one of his private beats. Breakfast is the only meal served and guest often dine at the nearby Anglers Arms. Up the curving staircase are three beautifully decorated guest bedrooms that enjoy idyllic views of a broad curve of the river. Apart from fishing there is plenty to keep visitors busy: the nearby coast of Antrim is full of cliffs, headlands, and a series of beautiful views. Visit Bushmills, famous for its whiskey, and walk the Giant's Causeway. At Cushendall you can detour into one of the nine glens of Antrim where the mountains run back parallel to each other, from the sea. *Directions:* From Coleraine take the A26 to Ballymoney and the B62 to the B66 signpost Garvah. Once on the B66 look for a signpost on your left Alternative route to Kilrea. Follow this road for 7 kilometers and you arrive at the Moore Lodge on your right beside the river (there is no sign, but tall stone gateposts and a driveway mark the entrance).

MOORE LODGE
Owners: Sir William and Lady Moore
Ballymoney
Co Antrim BT53 7NT
tel: (012665) 41043
3 ensuite rooms
From £32.50 per person B&B
Open May to August
Credit cards: none
Country house

Most of my family home would fit into the entrance hall of Temple House, but as a tour of the house subsequently displayed, that was just the tip of the iceberg, for beyond the enormous tiled entry hall with its array of wellington boots, fishing paraphernalia, and inclement weather gear lies a vast home with rooms of gigantic proportions. This is Sandy and Deb's family home and it's remarkable that they have made it into such a comfortable home. Those who are interested in the history of the place and wonderful stories of ancestors' exploits are directed to Sandy (he is extremely chemically sensitive so please refrain from using all scented products and aerosols). An air of warmth and faded elegance pervades this grand home that did not have electricity until 1962. All of the furniture made for the house is still here along with the original carpets and draperies, though Deb has added a lot of her own. Three of the bedrooms are gigantic. Realizing that guests enjoy the modern as well as the historic, bathrooms have been tucked into dressing rooms, good firm mattresses top historic beds, and central heating has been installed. Choose a pair of wellingtons and explore the estate from the vast parklands to the huge, walled vegetable garden that provides the fruit and vegetables served at meals partaken 'round the vast dining-room table. In an evening you can almost always be directed to Irish music and dancing. The Percevals can find enough to occupy your every waking moment that you will be obliged to stay for a month. *Directions:* From Sligo take the N4 to the N17 (Galway road). The house is signposted to the left.

TEMPLE HOUSE
Owners: Deb and Sandy Perceval
Ballymote
Co Sligo
tel: (071) 83329, fax: (071) 83808
5 rooms, 4 ensuite
From £33 per person B&B
Open Easter to November
Credit cards: EC, MC, VS
Country house

Ballinkeele House was built for the Maher family in 1840, and John and Margaret Maher are the fourth generation of Mahers to call Ballinkeele home. Set amidst 350 acres of park-like grounds, the house has all the solid quality of a grand home built in the early Victorian period: big rooms, fine ceilings, decorative doors, quality in every detail. Apart from the addition of heating and modern bathrooms, the house has not changed over the years. Soft oriental rugs grace the flagstone entry which is warmed by a huge, old-fashioned stove, grand oil paintings and family portraits adorn the walls. Antique furniture graces the cozy drawing room and enormous dining room where guests enjoy meals together round the large table. The Master Bedroom is a particularly large room decorated in soft red and beiges with a impressive four poster bed sitting center stage. There are walks through the estate and tennis can be played on the all-weather tennis court. The port of Rosslare is a 40-minute drive away, making Ballinkeele ideal for first or last nights in Ireland. Historic Wexford's Georgian theater is home to the October Opera Festival and on the outskirts of town is the Irish National Heritage Park with its reconstructions of old Irish buildings. *Directions:* From Dublin take the N11, Wexford road, to Gorey. Turn left opposite the 64 Lounge restaurant for Wexford (R741) for 30 kilometers and Ballinkeele House is signposted on your right.

BALLINKEELE HOUSE
Owners: Margaret and John Maher
Ballymurn
Enniscorthy
Co Wexford
tel: (053) 38105, fax: (053) 38468
5 room, 4 ensuite
From £30 per person B&B
Open March to 12 November
Credit cards: EC, MC, VS
Country house

Gregans Castle is only 70 kilometers from Shannon airport, so if you are heading north, this is the perfect spot to begin your stay in Ireland. This is not an imposing castle, but a sprawling manor house set in a lush green valley completely surrounded by the Burren, with its moonscapes of gray limestone and oasis of Alpine and Arctic plants. The entire house is delightfully decorated. Public rooms include a snug library and a cozy lounge—blazing turf fires add a cheery warmth. In the dining room, where Peter Haden supervises the production of delectable food, windows frame an outstanding view across the Burren to distant Galway Bay. My favorite room is the Corkscrew Bar with its blazing turf fire and blackened beams hung with copper and brass. Lunch is served here, and in the evening guests and locals gather for a drink and a chat. A new wing of traditional bedrooms and suites added in 1991 provide the most gracious accommodation. The older bedrooms are more modest in size, but comfortable and nicely decorated. Three large ground-floor suites overlook the garden. Local attractions include the Ailwee Caves, full of huge stalactites and stalagmites, and the 13-kilometers-long wall of the Cliffs of Moher. A 12½% service charge is added to your bill. *Directions:* From Shannon airport take the N18 to Ennis, the N85 towards Ennistymon, and the first right (R474) through Corofin. At the ruined castle turn right, and as you crest the Burren you see the hotel in the valley below.

GREGANS CASTLE
Owners: Moira, Peter, and Simon Haden
Ballyvaughan
Co Clare
tel: (065) 77005, fax: (065) 77111
22 ensuite rooms
Double from £115
Open Easter to mid-October
Credit cards: EC, MC, VS
Country house hotel

John and Mary Marnane have been welcoming visitors to their farm for over 20 years—Mary continues to offer a warm welcome with a cup of tea and encourages her guests to spend a couple of days with her so that she can get to know them and they can enjoy the peace and quiet of Irish farmhouse life. The seven simple bedrooms offer twin, double, and family accommodation, and several have small, modern shower rooms tucked into them. The upstairs bedroom at the back of the house is a particularly nice room. Mary offers good farmhouse-style dinners to guests seated round the large dining-room table. After dinner you can relax in the sitting room or take a walk down to the pub in the village. A big attraction for guests is son, Con's equestrian center which caters to every level of riding ability, from children (and adults) being led round the paddock to day-long treks through pretty countryside that overlooks the Glen of Aherlow and the Galtee Mountains. If you want to stay for a week, the Marnane's offer Primrose Cottage, a very attractive two bedroom residence nearby. Countryside drives include the Vee and the nearby Glen of Aherlow where you can enjoy the view, and woodland walks from Christ the King Statue. The Rock of Cashel, Hoare Abbey, Holy Cross Abbey, and Cahir Castle are all within a 19-kilometers radius. *Directions:* From Tipperary take the Waterford road (N24) to Bansha, turn left in the village and the farm is on your right after a kilometer.

BANSHA HOUSE
Owners: John and Mary Marnane
Bansha
Co Tipperary
tel: (062) 54194, fax: (062) 52499
7 rooms, 4 ensuite
From £15 per person B&B
Closed Christmas
Credit cards: EC, MC, VS
Farmhouse B&B

Just as you arrive in Bantry town, you see the entrance gate to Bantry House on your right Dating from 1750, this stately home has fine views of the bay, and like so many grand Irish homes, is struggling to keep up its elegant buildings. The current descendant of the Earls of Bantry, Egerton Shelswell-White, has tackled this problem by opening the house to the public who, with information sheets in hand, tour its lofty rooms and admire its elegant furniture, tapestries, and paintings, retiring afterwards to the tea shop in the old refectory. Yet this is a stately home with a difference, for one entire wing of the house and a couple of rooms over the tea shop have been restored in a more modern vein, offering large, bright, airy bedrooms (some with sitting rooms) on a bed-and-breakfast basis. After showing you to your room, the staff fade away until next morning when they prepare breakfast for you in the country-style dining room in what used to be the old cellars. In the evening you help yourselves to drinks from the honor bar, toast your toes by the fire, or if you wish, play billiards in the enormous billiard room. A tour of the house is included in the tariff, so you can pop through the concealed door into the long gallery to wander at leisure through the museum-like rooms of this grand old home. *Directions:* Bantry is on the N71 between Skibbereen and Kenmare.

BANTRY HOUSE
Owner: Egerton Shelswell-White
Bantry
Co Cork
tel: (027) 50047, fax: c/o (027) 50795
9 ensuite rooms
From £50 per person B&B
Open all year
Credit cards: all major
Country house

Rosemary and Brian McAuley had Dunauley designed to take advantage of the spectacular view of the island-dotted Bantry Bay, aptly framed by a wall of windows in the living/dining room. On a 1994 visit I was disappointed with the shabby decorational order of the exterior of the house, but then pleased to see that this did not extend to the interior. Guests enjoy both the living room and its particularly fine view as they sit 'round the fire in the evening and while tucking into an ample breakfast before setting out on a day's sightseeing. The bedrooms are prettily decorated with matching drapes and bedspreads. Three bedrooms share a large immaculate bathroom and downstairs an additional two have ensuite shower rooms (one of the downstairs rooms also enjoys a private entrance and small kitchen). Breakfast is the only meal Rosemary serves, but there are several restaurants in town for dinner. The drive from Bantry to Glengariff is a taste of the rugged landscape and exotic flora that you find in this part of Ireland. From the town you can take a boat to Garinish Island, a lush collection of interesting shrubs, trees, and flowers from all over the world. For over three years a hundred men worked to make Arran Bryce's garden, caseta, and temple, but financial hardships precluded the building of his home. *Directions:* From the center of Bantry follow white signs for the hospital through the one-way system and up the hill. Pass a church on the right and continue on this road till you see Dunauley signposted to the right—keep going uphill until you come to the house.

DUNAULEY
Owners: Rosemary and Brian McAuley
Seskin, Bantry
Co Cork
tel: (027) 50290
5 rooms, 2 ensuite
From £15.50 per person B&B
Open May to September
Credit cards: none
B&B

A long, shady driveway transports you from suburban Belfast to a haven with acres of immaculately landscaped gardens and a grand white Victorian home. Oakhill House has been May Noble's home for over 30 years and what an elegant home it is, filled with gorgeous antiques. Guests have the run of the house from the grand drawing room to the cozy television room with its comfy sofas and family photographs. The Green and Cream bedrooms are especially nicely decorated and enjoy enormous bathrooms. Every type of restaurant is to be found in Belfast, but if guests wish to join her for dinner, May will prepare a three-course meal and serve it in the stately dining room. May's great love, however, is not her beautiful home, but the acres of garden she has made from what once were fields. Now that her children are grown, the garden has become all-important and the swimming pool and tennis court sacrificed in favor of herbaceous borders and rose gardens. As well as being the expert on her own garden, May is a keen enthusiast of other people's, and she can recommend or arrange for you to visit nearby gardens. Belfast is largely a utilitarian city, and while you can appreciate the beauty of several of its old buildings, it is a city that endures. The Botanical Gardens, Queen's university and the museum are a world apart and just ten minutes from Oakhill. *Directions:* From Belfast take the A1 (Lisburn road) and go under the M1 to the suburb of Dunmurry where your turn left on Dunmurry Lane. The driveway for Oakhill House is on your right after 500 meters.

OAKHILL HOUSE
Owner: May Noble
59 Dunmurry Lane
Belfast BT17 9JR
tel: (01232) 610658, fax: (01232) 621566
4 ensuite rooms
Double from £70
Closed Christmas
Credit cards: none
Country house

The Gables was built by the owner of nearby Blarney Castle for the parish priest, and it served as a rectory until the Lynches purchased it as their family home in 1971. Berna and John Lynch offers guests a friendly welcome to their home and provide lots of information on Blarney. The Gables is decorated in a pleasing way, lovely antique furniture graces the large dining room, the welcoming lounge, and several of the bedrooms. The decor is old-fashioned and the beds a tad saggy. Accommodation is offered in two large family rooms with rather dated ensuite shower rooms and a small double room that uses the adjacent old-fashioned bathroom with a huge tub. There are many activities to occupy you in nearby Blarney besides the obligatory visit to the castle to kiss the Blarney stone: an excellent riding school is five minutes way, golf fifteen minutes, and the shopping in Blarney is excellent, with the stores staying open till dusk during the summer months. There are several places to eat in town, but if you make arrangements in advance, Berna is happy to offer you a traditional Irish dinner. *Directions:* The Gables is signposted on the outskirts of the village on the main Cork to Blarney road. If you are arriving from Killarney, drive through the village onto the Cork road and take the second turn to the left for the 3-kilometer drive to the Gables.

THE GABLES
Owners: Berna and John Lynch
Stoneview
Blarney
Co Cork
tel: (021) 385330
3 rooms, 2 ensuite
From £15.50 per person B&B
Open March to October
Credit cards: none
B&B

Bobbie Smith is a caring hostess, carrying on the tradition of warm farmhouse hospitality started by her mother many years ago. Bobbie is an unpretentious, warm, and fun person and her home reflects her welcoming, easygoing personality. Filled with mellow old furniture, books, pictures, and family mementos, the Old Rectory is very much a comfortable family home for Bobbie, her New Zealand-born husband Don, and their three daughters. Guests are welcomed with a reviving pot of tea in the drawing room, and it is here that they chat with fellow guests before dinner which is taken by candlelight round the long, gleaming dining-room table. Bedrooms have the same traditional family feel—ask for the one with the large feather mattress, its comfort will surprise you. It is a quiet and peaceful area perfect for cycling, so Don organizes cycling holidays which include cycle hire, airport pickup, and baggage transportation. Those who prefer to stick to their car for sightseeing explorations will find Kilkenny with its castle, fine old shops, and lovely buildings just a twenty-minute drive away. Day trips can be taken to Waterford, of crystal fame, Kildare to visit the national stud and Japanese Gardens, and Glendalough with its ancient monastic ruins. *Directions:* Take the N9 from Dublin to Royal Oak (south of Carlow), turn left into Bagenalstown (Muine Bheag), and right in the village for the 6-kilometer drive to Lorum Old Rectory.

LORUM OLD RECTORY
Owners: Bobbie and Don Smith
Kilgreaney, Bagenalstown
Borris
Co Carlow
tel: (0503) 75282, fax: (0503) 75455
5 rooms, 4 ensuite
From £22.50 per person B&B
Open all year
Credit cards: EC, MC, VS
Country house

Bruckless House was built in the mid-18th century and lived in by the Cassidy brothers, traders and merchants who took pickled herring from Dunkineely, traded some for arms and ammunition in Sligo, then went on down to Portugal where they sold the guns to Napoleon and pickled herrings to Wellington. Later the house was owned by a passionate communist, Commander Fforde, who is remembered for his many good works in the area. Continuing the tradition of colorful owners, Clive and Joan Evans and their family moved here after spending many years in Hong Kong. This lovely home has the most marvelous location set in wooded acres with garden paths leading down to the rocky shoreline of Bruckless Bay. Colorful Oriental rugs warm the flagstone entryway and mementos of the Evans' years abroad blend with comfortable family antiques. A log fire warms the dining room on chilly mornings as guests breakfast together 'round the long polished table. Breakfast is the only meal served as there are restaurants in every price range nearby. Up the narrow back staircase, a two single and a small double room, each with matching print duvets and curtains, share a large bathroom with a huge, old-fashioned tub and shower. A larger twin bedded room has an ensuite bathroom. At the top of the driveway, an adorable two bedroom lodge is perfect for families who wish to stay for several days; in the summer it is let on a weekly basis. Bruckless is ideally placed for exploring Donegal. *Directions:* From Donegal take the N56 towards Killybegs. Bruckless House is on the left in the village of Bruckless.

BRUCKLESS HOUSE
Owners: Clive and Joan Evans
Bruckless
Co Donegal
tel: (073) 37071, fax: (073) 37070
4 rooms, 1 ensuite
From £20 per person B&B
Open April to September
Credit cards: EC, MC, VS
B&B

Clohamon House has a wonderfully relaxed informality—it really is a place to dedicate a stay of several days to, for beyond the luxurious house lie some really pretty grounds full of badgers and foxes. There are also Connemara ponies, for Maria has a famous stud of ponies and is an international judge of the breed. Maria and Richard are friendly, amusing hosts and their home has an enviable collection of antiques, for not only does it contain Richard's family furniture and portraits, but when Maria came here she added heirlooms from her ancestral home, Waterford Castle. Maria is happy to provide dinner on all but Sunday nights, and guests dine together 'round the candlelit dining room table. I particularly enjoyed Ashstand, a large twin bedroom with a panoramic view of the Slaney valley and Sinnotts, an elegant, four-poster room. Less expensive accommodation is offered in Dairymaids, a tiny, two-room cottage. If you want to stay for a week there's a well-equipped, self-catering cottage across the stableyard. You can cycle the lanes (bicycles are available), go horse riding nearby, birdwatching, and walking, or take to your car and visit Kilkenny, Waterford, Wicklow, and Carlow. *Directions:* Bunclody is on the main Carlow to Enniscorthy road (N80). From Carlow turn left at the crossroads in Bunclody, cross the river and at the 'Y' junction go right up the hill. Halfway up the hill turn right and Clohamon House is on your right after 1 kilometer.

CLOHAMON HOUSE   **NEW**
Owners: Sir Richard and Lady (Maria) Levinge
Bunclody
Co Wexford
tel: (054) 77235, fax fax: (054) 77956
4 ensuite rooms
From £42 per person B&B
Open March to mid-November
Credit cards: EC, MC, VS
Country house

The Bushmills Inn was in a very sad and sorry state before it was rescued by Roy Bolton and Richard Wilson who have transformed it into a traditional Ulster hostelry. A rocking chair sits before an enormous fireplace and displays of old plates adorn the mantle. The ambiance of an old coaching inn continues to the restaurant with its whitewashed stone walls and tall pine settles dividing the room into intimate little areas. The old bar and kitchen have been transformed into the Brasserie, a traditional, Victorian-style eating house with a long bar and little tables and chairs—all illuminated by flickering gaslight. The well priced menu offers casual bistro-type food and you may well want to start or end your meal with a dram from the distillery up the road— Bushmills is famous for its whiskey and on weekdays you can take a tour of the distillery. The bedrooms are on the small side, attractively decorated, and each accompanied by a tiny shower room. If you enjoy more space, request Room 24. You may have the pleasure of seeing your nation's flag flown in your honor as the inn has the charming custom of raising the national flag of their resident who is from farthest away. Nearby are 13th-century Dunluce Castle and the Giant's Causeway. *Directions:* From Coleraine take the B19 to Bushmills. As you enter the town turn left along Main Street and the hotel is on your left.

THE BUSHMILLS INN
Owners: Roy Bolton and Richard Wilson
25 Main Street
Bushmills
Co Antrim BT57 8QA
tel: (012657) 32339, fax: (012657) 32048
11 ensuite rooms
Double from £68
Open all year
Credit cards: all major
Inn

Tired of the city life, Mike and Barbara Barrett looked around for an alternate lifestyle—and after much thought decided to start a deer farm. With the farm they selected, came a rabbit warren of a bed and breakfast that inspired them to broaden their horizons into the hospitality market. Out went the tiny partitioned bedrooms and in their place are two large twin rooms with sparkling shower rooms, a large double with bathroom, and a single room with bathroom down the hall. Simple decor and orthopedic beds are the order of the day. Guests have the use of a cozy sitting room at the heart of the house and a small conservatory. Breakfast is a hearty repast. A reader has written praising Barbara's homecooked dinners and lauding the Barretts for their warm hospitality. As an alternative to eating in, guests can drive 11 kilometers to The Neptune in Ballyhack or the Mariners Inn in New Ross. The adjacent John F. Kennedy Park is a landscaped park with trees from around the world. As a bonus, Mike usually takes guests out to feed the gentle deer on his farm. Park View Farm is only a 40-kilometers drive from Rosslare Harbor, making it ideal for your first nights in Ireland if your are arriving by ferry from Wales or France. *Directions:* From Rosslare or Wexford take the Cork road (N25). At the Burmah Petrol station in Ballinaboola, turn left, following signposts for John F. Kennedy Park—10 kilometers. Park View Farm is 1 kilometer from the park entrance.

PARK VIEW FARM
Owners: Barbara and Mike Barrett
Campile
Co Wexford
tel: (051) 388178
4 rooms, 3 ensuite
From £17.50 per person B&B
Open May to September
Credit cards: none
Farmhouse B&B

Flower-filled woodlands line the driveway leading to Glendalough House, a charming Victorian hunting lodge overlooking beautiful Caragh Lake. Josephine Roder is your warm, welcoming hostess assisted by her son Alex, when he is home on school holidays. Josephine's family is completed by Henry, the peacock (who has a penchant for perching atop cars); Fionn, the friendly Dalmatian, Jasper, the darting Jack Russell, and Pushkin, the affectionate cat. A stay of several days gives you the opportunity to get to know the family, partake of candlelit dinners, and explore the area. While all the bedrooms are most attractively furnished with antiques, three are particularly attractive because of their delightful views through the treetops to the lake and distant mountains. A ground floor bedroom is perfect for those who have difficulty with stairs (bathroom across the hall). Behind the house, two bedrooms are found on either side of a comfortable sitting room in what was formerly the stables. This is an idyllic spot perfectly located for forays to the Ring of Kerry, the Dingle Peninsula, and Killarney. Our favorite (clear-day) drive takes you through narrow lanes across the rugged McGillcuddy Reeks (Ireland's highest mountains) to Blackwater Bridge and Kenmare. *Directions:* From Killorglin take the N70 towards Cahersiveen for 5 kilometers. Turn left signposted Glendalough House and Caragh Lake. Glendalough House is at the end of this road on the right.

GLENDALOUGH HOUSE **NEW**
Owner: Josephine Roder-Bradshaw
Caragh Lake
Co Kerry
tel: (066) 69156, fax: (066) 69156
7 rooms, 6 ensuite
From £38 per person B&B
Closed December
Credit cards: EC, MC, VS
Country house

The Londonderry Arms was built in 1848 as a coaching inn by the Marchioness of Londonderry. Her great-grandson, Sir Winston Churchill, inherited it in 1921. Frank and Moira O'Neill bought the hotel in 1947, and now it is in the capable hands of their son, Frank, who has taken care to retain the old-world charm of the ivy covered building. The old bull's eye panes of glass and dark carved furniture in the dining room and library reflect this. Guests gather in the back lounge for tea and scones or retire to the front sitting room to read. The Old Coach House Bar is popular with the locals who enjoy a game of bar billiards as well as convivial conversation. Upstairs the bedrooms are very plainly decorated, though a recent visit saw improvements in the drapes and general decor. Quite the nicest room is Room Two, a large corner room with a distant sea view and heavy, highly polished antique furniture. Running northward from Larne to the world famous Giant's Causeway is the Antrim Coast where the road hugs the sea and nine glens (valleys which run inland from the sea) offer diverse scenery. The coast road's sheer cliffs, rocky headlands and succession of stunning views are breathtaking. The hotel has bicycles for guests and maps that outline scenic walks. *Directions:* Carnlough is 56 kilometers north of Belfast. If you are arriving from County Donegal, take the A2 to Coleraine, the A26 to Ballymena, and the A42 to Carnlough.

LONDONDERRY ARMS
Owner: Frank O'Neill
Manager: Mary O'Neil
Carnlough
Co Antrim BT44 0EU
tel: (01574) 885255, fax: (01574) 885263
21 ensuite rooms
Double from £65
Open all year
Credit cards: all major
Inn

Glencarne House is one of those welcoming places that guests love to return to, for Agnes Harrington is the most hospitable of hostesses. There is nothing fancy or decorator perfect about the decor, but Agnes takes great pride in keeping everything spotless and adding homey touches. Agnes is particularly proud that her bed and breakfast has won three national awards. The perfume of flowers blends with that of the furniture polish used to keep the lovely old furniture gleaming bright. A hearty farmhouse dinner is served 'round the large dining-room table—the vegetables, fruits, lamb, and beef are fresh from the farm and carefully cooked by Agnes. All but one of the bedrooms have ensuite bathrooms—one, a family room, has two lovely old brass and iron beds and the large front bedroom has a beautiful brass and iron bed and a child's bed in the bathroom/dressing room. There are many places to go and things to see in the area—in Carrick on Shannon, you can rent a cabin cruiser and meander along the River Shannon and her lakes, stopping off to visit the villages and their pubs along the way. *Directions:* Glencarne House is on the N4, Dublin to Sligo road, between Carrick on Shannon and Boyle.

GLENCARNE HOUSE
Owners: Agnes and Pat Harrington
Carrick on Shannon
Co Roscommon
tel: (079) 67013
6 rooms, 5 ensuite
From £16 per person B&B
Open March to October
Credit cards: none
Farmhouse B&B

Hollywell is a lovely old house set in a large garden overlooking the River Shannon. It has a secluded riverside location, just a couple of minutes' walk to the heart of Carrick on Shannon, a lively riverside town which is a major terminus for weekly boat hire on the Shannon. For six generations, Tom Maher's family were the proprietors of the Bush Hotel, and now Tom and Rosaleen keep up the family's tradition for hospitality by welcoming guests into their home. Guests have a large sitting room with comfy sofas, books, games, and TV where they gather round the fire in the evening. Breakfast is the only meal served at the little tables arranged 'round the grand piano in the dining room, but there is no shortage of places to eat dinner in town. Three grandfather clocks grace the hallways and a sofa and books are grouped at the head of the stairs to take advantage of the view over a broad stretch of the River Shannon. The two large front bedrooms share the same lovely view, while the back bedrooms are small only in comparison to those at the front. Fishing is a popular pastime hereabouts and you can enjoy walks along the canals. The nearby Forest Park is found on the grounds of the former Rockingham House. The park's amenities include nature trails, a bog garden, and the relics of the former mansion. *Directions*: Take the N4 (Sligo road) from Dublin to Carrick on Shannon. Cross the river, turn up the hill by Gings Pub, and Hollywell is on your left.

HOLLYWELL   **NEW**
Owners: Rosaleen and Tom Maher
Liberty Hill
Carrick on Shannon
Co Roscommon
tel: (078) 21124, fax: (078) 21124
4 ensuite rooms
From £25 per person B&B
Open March to November
Credit cards: none
B&B

Ardmayle is a very old country farmhouse that has been owned by the De Vere Hunt family since 1840. The great attractions of staying here are that you can participate in life on a working farm with cows, sheep, and horses and enjoy trout fishing on a 2-kilometer stretch of the River Suir (no extra cost). Annette offers a warm welcome with tea and scones, and youngest son Evan will take you on a tour of the farm. The good-value-for-money dinners are delicious and include a starter, homemade soup, main course with fresh vegetables, dessert, and coffee. The three nicest bedrooms have ensuite bathrooms, while the other two share a large bathroom with an old-fashioned claw-foot tub. For an evening out, Annette can often direct you to local pubs that offer traditional Irish music (be warned: it begins late). If you want to venture beyond the farm, Cashel with its famous rock, is just 7 kilometers of narrow country lanes away. An hour's drive brings you to Kilkenny, Cahir Castle, and the scenic drive across the Vee. *Directions:* Leave Cashel towards Dublin (N8). When you get to the Dublin road do not take it, but keep left down the hill. At the bottom of the hill (a confusing three-lane junction) take the left fork for 7 kilometers through the village of Ardmayle. Outside the village, turn left at a T-junction. The first entrance on the right is to Ardmayle House.

ARDMAYLE HOUSE   **NEW**
Owners: Annette Hunt and family
Ardmayle
Cashel
Co Tipperary
tel: (0504) 42399, fax: (0504) 42420
5 rooms, 3 ensuite
From £15 per person B&B
Open May to October
Credit cards: none
Farmhouse B&B

The setting for Cashel House is spectacularly impressive: at the head of Cashel Bay with Cashel Hill standing guard behind, a solid white house nestles amongst acres and acres of woodland and gardens of exotic flowering shrubs from all over the world. Kilometers of garden footpaths are yours to wander along, and the beautiful seashore is yours to explore. This is not the kind of hotel to spend just a night in—once you have settled into your lovely room and sampled the exquisite food in the spectacular conservatory dining room, you will be glad that you have made Cashel House the base for your Connemara explorations. Graceful antiques, turf fires, and lovely arrangements of freshly picked flowers create a warm, country-house welcome. It feels particularly decadent to have breakfast served to you in bed on a prettily decorated tray. All the bedrooms are beautifully furnished and decorated, each accompanied by a sparkling bathroom. Thirteen exquisite suites occupy a more modern wing and enjoy comfortable sitting areas overlooking the garden. Tennis rackets are available so keen tennis players can enjoy the court that borders the bay. Riding lessons and treks are a big feature for many guests—I had dinner with an Italian couple who were spending a week's vacation with riding activities for their young daughters and golf for themselves. Beyond this sheltered spot Connemara is yours to explore. A 12½% service charge is added to your bill. *Directions:* Take the N59 from Galway (towards Clifden) through Oughterard and turn left to the village of Cashel 2 kilometers after Recess. The hotel is on the shore just after the church.

CASHEL HOUSE
Owners: Kay and Dermot McEvilly
Cashel, Connemara
Co Galway
tel: (095) 31001, fax: (095) 31077
32 ensuite rooms
Double from £141.75
Open all year
Credit cards: all major
Country house hotel

While it looks like a modern house of rather dubious architectural merit from outside, when you enter Wandesforde House you realize that you are in an old building. I was surprised to learn that it was built as a school by the Countess of Ormonde in 1824, for the children of the Castlecomer estate. It continued as a school until the 1970s, then lay empty for some years until it was bought by Phil and David Fleming and converted into a B&B and their family home. One of the two large classrooms is now a cheerful sitting and dining room with groupings of small chairs and tables. Phil always asks her guests what they would like for dinner and there is always a choice of meat and fish for a main course. If you arrive without having made a dinner reservation, it is usually not a problem for her to provide soup and a sandwich. The six small bedrooms are found either on the ground floor or up a narrow flight of stairs, and each has a compact shower room. Rooms come in a combination of twins and doubles and are unsuitable for large suitcases. Within a twenty-minute drive are Kilkenny city, Carlow, the Barrow and Nore valleys, and the Slieve Bloom Mountains. Kilkenny is renowned for its crafts, particularly in pottery, glass and leather. *Directions:* From Kilkenny take the N78 through Castlecomer towards Naas and Wandesforde House is on your right after 6 kilometers.

WANDESFORDE HOUSE **NEW**
Owners: Phil and David Fleming
Moneenroe
Castlecomer
Co Kilkenny
tel: (056) 42441
6 ensuite rooms
From £18 per person B&B
Closed Christmas
Credit cards: EC, MC, VS
Guesthouse

Ballyvolane House sits comfortably in a magnificent setting of gardens and wooded grounds—a grand old mansion, home to Merrie and Jeremy Green. Merrie is an ardent fisherwoman and takes every opportunity to go fishing, though Jeremy says that she usually just points guests in the right direction (she has 16 rods of salmon fishing). He also claims that their croquet lawn is the most challenging in Ireland—cheating to win is encouraged. Guests soon realize that Jeremy's unselfconscious humor, and Merrie's straightforward sense of fun are applied to everything, which certainly means that guests to this gracious mansion do not walk around talking in hushed whispers: a happy camaraderie pervades the place. This is a friendly, happy house where guests wander in and out of the kitchen, which is in a vast, tall-ceilinged, drawing-type of room. After drinks in the drawing room guests gather for dinner round the long polished table watched over by a parade of benevolent ancestors. One of the lovely bedrooms has a bath so deep that you have to step up to get into it. Within a radius of a few kilometers there are no fewer than eleven golf courses and within an hour's drive are Blarney, with its famous castle, Cork City, Fota House with its magnificent collection of paintings, and the bustling fishing and boating town of Kinsale. *Directions:* From Fermoy take the N8 towards Cork to Rathcormac where the 6-kilometer drive to Ballyvolane House is signposted to your left

BALLYVOLANE HOUSE
Owners: Merrie and Jeremy Green
Castlelyons
Co Cork
tel: (025) 36349, fax: (025) 36781
7 rooms, 5 ensuite
From £35 per person B&B
Open all year
Credit cards: all major
Country house

Families stopping at Lisnamandra on their way north have been known to go no farther, contenting themselves with whiling away the hours in this peaceful spot and enjoying the warm farmhouse hospitality that Bert and Iris Neill offer. Downstairs the dining and sitting rooms are large and comfortable with high ceilings, decorated in a hodge-podge style of modern and traditional. Upstairs, the bedrooms are prettily papered and decorated and most have a small shower room ensuite. A large chest in the upstairs hallway contains extra pillows, blankets, and towels and guests are encouraged to help themselves to additional supplies. Iris offers a traditional, four-course farmhouse dinner and breakfast from a menu that includes freshly squeezed juice, pancakes, waffles, omelets, kippers, and a cheese and meat plate as alternatives to the traditional Irish breakfast. Lisnamandra is a ten-minute drive from Lough Oughter, a vast complex of lakes and rivers that delights championship and amateur fishermen with good catches of bream and roach. Even if you don't fish, Lisnamandra is a place to visit for warm farmhouse hospitality, good home cooking, and countryside tranquillity. Tours can be taken of the nearby Cavan crystal factory. *Directions:* Lisnamandra farmhouse is 8 kilometers south of Cavan on the L15 (R198), 2 kilometers before you reach the village of Crossdoney.

LISNAMANDRA
Owners: Iris and Bert Neill
Crossdoney
Cavan
Co Cavan
tel: (049) 37196
6 rooms, 4 ensuite
From £14 per person B&B
Open April to September
Credit cards: none
Farmhouse B&B

With its close proximity to Shannon airport, Carnelly House makes an ideal first or last night's stay in Ireland. Dramatically set at the end of a long driveway, this grand Queen-Anne-style Georgian residence offers the most spacious, luxury accommodation at grand hotel prices. On arrival, guests are offered tea or coffee in the large drawing room where softly painted paneled walls and slipcovered chairs present an inviting picture. Guests sip pre-dinner drinks here under the ornate La Francini plasterwork ceiling. Apparently the Francini brothers labored for over a year on the delicate tracery and were paid for their efforts in Irish whiskey. Dinner is wonderful and the service personnel are as charming and competent as any you will encounter. Up the grand staircase are the very large bedrooms, with old paneled walls painted in soft pastels that coordinate with elegant drapes and fitted bedspreads. Each bedroom has a very large bathroom which is nothing short of splendid. Bunratty Folk park with its interesting old Irish cottages and houses is just down the road with its adjacent, landmark pub, Durty Nellys. The Burren, Ailwee caves, Cliffs of Moher, and Yeats's home, Thoor Ballylee, are also worth a visit. *Directions:* From Shannon airport take the N18 towards Ennis and Galway. Watch for Dromoland Castle on your right: Carnelly House is 4 kilometers from Dromoland's gates on your left (after you go under the pylons watch for the entrance at the end of an old estate wall).

CARNELLY HOUSE **NEW**
Owners: Rosemarie and Dermott Gleeson
Clarecastle
Co Clare
tel: (0365) 28442, fax: (0365) 29222
5 ensuite rooms
From £73 per person B&B
Closed December
Credit cards: EC, MC, VS
Country house

Mal Dua is not included because of its architectural merits (it's a modern bungalow with flower-filled swans on the gateposts and concrete gnomes on the patio), but because it has attractive, tastefully decorated bedrooms and welcoming owners in Kathleen and Ivor Duane. The house's unusual name is a combination of its owners surnames, Maloney and Duane. The sunny lobby doubles as a sitting room with sofas and chairs in deep pink velour that match the carpet and the balloon shades. Breakfast is the only meal served in the small breakfast room, though plans are afoot to extend the property and add a residents' lounge and restaurant. All but the tiny single bedroom are spacious and come with different combinations of double and single beds. All have a shower, hair dryer, TV, phone, trouser press, and tea and coffee makings. The decor is very attractive, with pastel-painted walls and coordinating drapes and bedspreads. There are restaurants aplenty just up road in the lively little town of Clifden. During the third week in August, Clifden hosts the Connemara Pony Show and rooms are at a premium. *Directions:* Take the N59 from Galway to the outskirts of Clifden. Mal Dua is on your right as you enter the town.

MAL DUA   **NEW**
Owners: Kathleen and Ivor Duane
Galway Road
Clifden
Co Galway
tel: (095) 21171, fax: (095) 21739
11 ensuite rooms
From £20 per person B&B
Open March to November
Credit cards: EC, MC, VS
B&B

The harbormaster certainly picked a pretty site for his home on the quay, with its wide vista of the inlet of Ardbear Bay and the town of Clifden winding up the hillside. Since 1820, Quay House has served variously as the harbormaster's home, a convent, a monastery, and a hotel. Paddy and Julia bought the house and the adjacent cottage in almost derelict condition, giving them a new lease on life as a stylish B&B and bistro-style restaurant. They decorated the whole in a refreshingly eclectic style, blending old, modern, and unconventional in an idiosyncratic way with little jokes and quirks such as vegetarian alley, a corridor of hunting trophies, and the wall of prints with one hung upside down. In the restaurant, little tables are topped with paper tablecloths and there's a short a-la-carte menu with and a keenly priced wine list. Upstairs, the bedrooms vary in size from spacious, high-ceilinged rooms to under-the-eaves cozy. Several are very "traditional country house" in their decor, others light, fresh, and more bohemian. Some have showers, and others clawfoot tubs and showers. A stroll brings you into the lively town of Clifden. It's a pretty spot and there is so much to see and do in Connemara that it merits a stay of several days. *Directions:* Take the N59 from Galway to Clifden and follow the one-way system to the top of the town where you take lower fork at the first 'Y' down onto the quay. Quay House is on your right.

THE QUAY HOUSE **NEW**
Owners: Julia and Paddy Foyle
Beach Road
Clifden
Co Galway
tel: (095) 21369, fax: (095) 41168
7 ensuite rooms
From £20 per person B&B
Open March to November
Credit cards: EC, MC, VS
B&B

Rock Glen is a cozy hotel converted from an 18th-century hunting lodge with all the outdoor beauties of Connemara at its doorstep. Enjoy the delights of the area, safe in the certainty that a warm welcome, superlative food, and a snug retreat await you on your return to Rock Glen. An inviting grouping of plump chairs around a turf fire, the chatter of locals and guests, and the warmth of the adjacent sunlounge invite you to linger in the bar. The dining room, decked out in shades of gold and pink, its tables laid with silver, complements the fine cuisine supervised by John Roche who trained as a chef in the prestigious Ashford Castle. Evangeline also worked at Ashford and it is at Rock Glen where they have put to work their professional training, creating a countryside hotel that recalls the pleasures of a leisurely and more sedate way of life. The small, comfortable bedrooms are uniform in size and decorated in pastel shades, all well kitted out with trouser press, hairdryer, and TV. If you book early, you may secure a room with a distant sea view. Quite the nicest room is the most expensive, number 35, a two-bedroom suite with a spacious sitting area and private balcony overlooking the sea. The hotel also has a full-sized snooker table and an all-weather tennis court. A 12½% service charge is added to your bill. Connemara's stunning scenery is on your doorstep. *Directions:* Take the N59 from Galway to Clifden, then just after passing the church turn left towards Ballyconeely. Rock Glen is to your right about 1 kilometer from town.

ROCK GLEN HOTEL
Owners: Evangeline and John Roche
Clifden, Connemara
Co Galway
tel: (095) 21035, fax: (095) 21737
30 ensuite rooms
Double from £90
Open March to October
Credit cards: all major
Country house hotel

Blackheath House was built as a rectory in 1795, its most famous incumbent being the Reverend Alexander, whose wife Cecile wrote many famous hymns including "There is a Green Hill Far Away," "All Things Bright and Beautiful," and "Once in Royal David's City." Joe and Margaret Erwin returned to Ireland in 1978 to convert Margaret's family home into a country house hotel and restaurant. The drawing room offers a lovely collection of family furniture and a grand piano. Guests dine downstairs in the cellar restaurant, MacDuff's, where a comfortable, bistro-style atmosphere prevails and dining is a la carte. Margaret puts a great deal of care into her cooking. Dining is at a leisurely pace and the service is most attentive. Upstairs, the bedrooms are stylishly decorated and furnished with antiques. All are equipped with color televisions and modern bathrooms. From this quiet country spot, venture out to explore the scenic Antrim coast with its headlands and stunning views, and its most famous attraction, the Giant's Causeway. You can detour into one of the nine glens of Antrim, and visit nearby Bushmills where you can tour the world's oldest whiskey distillery. *Directions:* If you are arriving in Northern Ireland from County Donegal, take the N13 from Letterkenny to Derry. Cross the Foyle Bridge and at Limavady take the A37 towards Coleraine, turn right on the A29 (Garvagh and Cookstown road) for 6 kilometers then turn right on a small road (Mascosquin). Blackheath House is on your right.

BLACKHEATH HOUSE
Owners: Margaret and Joseph Erwin
112 Killeague Road
Blackhill, Coleraine
Co Londonderry, BT51 4HN
tel: (01265) 868433
5 ensuite rooms
Double from £60
Open all year
Credit cards: EC, MC, VS
Country house hotel

I arrived at Camus House on a picture-perfect spring day when the cherry trees were a drift of blossom and the old ivy-covered house, which dates back to 1685, a mass of pink clematis. The speculation is that the house, sitting next to an ancient churchyard with a high cross, was built on the site of a monastery. It is a peaceful spot on a quiet byway just off the busy A54 overlooking the lazily meandering River Bann. With its close proximity to the river, it is no wonder that fishing is a family passion: Josephine King fishes at every opportunity and her daughter, Trish, was on the Irish fishing team. If guests have permits, they too can go fishing. Josephine is particularly fond of blue, so has decked out her dining room with a royal blue carpet, displays blue and white china on her large dresser, blue bottleware on her mantelpiece, and guests enjoy breakfast (the only meal served) on blue dishes. For dinner they often go into Coleraine or to the nearby Brown Trout. The three bedrooms share a family bathroom upstairs and a shower room downstairs. All are prettily decorated in pastels and have a TV, tea makings, and electric blankets. Camus House is a perfect base for visiting the Antrim Coast. *Directions:* Take the Kilrea (A54) exit from the second roundabout in Coleraine. Follow this road for 4 kilometers and immediately as the forest park on your left ends the driveway to Camus House is on your right (before you come to the river).

CAMUS HOUSE   **NEW**
Owner: Josephine King
27 Curragh Road (A54)
Coleraine
Co Londonderry
tel: (01265) 42982
3 rooms sharing 2 bathrooms
From £18 per person B&B
Open all year
Credit cards: none
Farmhouse B&B

The charm of Greenhill House is Elizabeth Hegarty, who is exceptionally sweet and helpful. I very much enjoy the late evening conversation around the drawing room fire with a cup of tea and cakes, while James and Elizabeth and fellow guests are "putting the world to rights." All this after a 6:30 pm dinner that includes a groaning dessert trolley where Elizabeth encourages you to try a bit of everything (wine is not served). The lovely farmhouse is lovingly decorated with antiques, and bouquets of fresh garden flowers adding the finishing touches. Our bedroom (overlooking an immaculate garden) had everything: sightseeing information; a tray set with teapot, kettle, tea bags, coffee, and chocolate; hairdryer; television; and even a little box of After Eight Mints by the bedside. Plump comforters top the beds and fluffy towels hang on the old-fashioned towel rail, all coordinating in shades of pink with the curtains and the carpet. Bedrooms in the attic have bathrooms tucked neatly under the eaves while other rooms have snug shower rooms, in what at first appears to be large fitted closets. It goes without saying that you should plan on staying here for several days. With Greenhill House as a base you can set off to explore the Antrim coast. *Directions:* If you are arriving from County Donegal, follow the same driving directions as for Blackheath House, but continue along the A29 for 11 kilometers, turning left on the B66 towards Ballymoney.

GREENHILL HOUSE
Owners: James and Elizabeth Hegarty
24 Greenhill Road
Aghadowey, Coleraine
Co Londonderry, BT51 4EU
tel: (01265) 868241
6 ensuite rooms
From £21 per person B&B
Open March to October
Credit cards: EC, MC, VS
Farmhouse B&B

Ashford Castle was built over a period of 30 years by Lord Ardilaun in the 19th century. Incorporated into its castellated facade are the remains of the 13th-century de Burgo Castle and the original Ashford House, built in the style of a French chateau. This certainly was a sumptuous residence. In more recent years, Ashford has been renovated and luxuriously appointed to create one of Europe's premier castle hotels. The decor of the public rooms is lavish and opulent, the views across the lake stunning. This is a hotel that attracts kings and presidents—the billiard room was built for King Edward VII when he came to stay in 1905; for President Reagan's visit in 1984, a luxurious bed was commissioned. No meals are included in the quoted tariff. After a splendid dinner in one of the castle's two restaurants, you can enjoy Irish entertainment in the Dungeon Bar, take a stroll through the lakeside gardens or saunter into the adjacent village of Cong. The setting on the shores of beautiful Lough Corrib, with its hundreds of islands, bays, and coves is stunning. A nine-hole golf course and tennis courts are reserved for guests' use. The Lough is famous for its fishing and shooting for snipe and woodcock can be arranged. *Directions:* The castle is 43 kilometers north of Galway on the shores of Lough Corrib. Inform the gatekeeper that you are staying at the castle and you will not be charged for entrance.

ASHFORD CASTLE
Manager: Rory Murphy
Cong
Co Mayo
tel: (092) 46003, fax: (092) 46260
83 ensuite rooms
Double from £195
Open all year
Credit cards: all major
Luxury resort

Ballykine House was built as a gamekeeper's lodge when nearby Ashford Castle was the country home of the Guinness family. Now it is Ann and Barry Lambe's home, and while he works for the forestry department, Ann welcomes guests to their home. You enter from a small hallway into the pretty pink parlor where plump chairs are drawn invitingly 'round the fire. It's a cozy place to sit on a chilly evening, though Ann finds that guests often prefer the large conservatory that overlooks the front garden. Up the narrow stairs are four neatly decorated bedrooms, each with a double and a single bed and a small shower room tucked into the corner. Breakfast is the only meal served, but there are several restaurants to choose from in nearby Cong. If you want to visit Ashford Castle, Ann can outline a country walk that takes you the 8 kilometers to the grandiose castle set on the shores of Lough Corrib. Combine this with a boat trip to the islands on the lough and you have a very pleasant summer day's outing. Beyond the village of Clonbur, the narrow road brings you to vistas of the island-dotted Lough Corrib, with magnificent mountains rising in the background. *Directions:* Cong is 43 kilometers north of Galway on the shores of Lough Corrib. From Cong take the R345 towards Clonbur and Ballykine House is on your right before you reach the village of Clonbur.

BALLYKINE HOUSE
Owners: Ann and Barry Lambe
Clonbur
Cong
Co Galway
tel: (092) 46150
From £14 per person B&B
4 ensuite rooms
Open from April to October
Credit cards: none
Farmhouse B&B

Maura and Michael Verling have long been collectors of antique furniture, and when Maura decided that she wanted to try her hand at B&B, they looked around for an old home to house their collection. They found the ideal spot, for Conna House, with its well proportioned Victorian rooms and stripped-pine doors and floors, is the perfect backdrop for all her treasures. Toast your toes by the fire in the cluttered parlor and enjoy a drink with your hosts. Dinner is a hearty repast: on the night of my visit we had smoked salmon and salad, tomato soup, breast of chicken with fresh veggies, and dessert—concluded with Irish coffee by the fire. Conna House is a very casual place, and guests often wander into the farmhouse kitchen for tea and a chat 'round the pine table. Upstairs, the bedrooms are delightfully decorated in a less cluttered way than downstairs, and several have lovely, old, pine furniture. A half-hour drive brings you to the city of Cork. Midleton is the home of the Jameson whiskey distillery where you can watch a film on the making of Irish whiskey, then taste some samples and enjoy the craft and coffee shop. Nearby in Cobh, the Heritage Centre covers Irish emigration, the *Lusitania* (which sank offshore), and the *Titanic* (Cobh was its last port of call). *Directions:* From Fermoy take the Cork road (N8) through Rathcormac to the Bride River bridge: turn left and next left. The house is 10 kilometers from the N8 on the right before you reach Conna.

CONNA HOUSE   **NEW**
Owners: Maura and Michael Verling
Conna
Co Cork
tel: (058) 59419
4 ensuite rooms
From £22 per person B&B
Open March to December
Credit cards: none
B&B

Fergus View is a perfect stepping-off place for those arriving at Shannon airport and heading north, but stretch your visit to several nights so that you can explore the area. Fergus View was built as a teacher's residence at the turn of the century and Declan's grandfather was its first occupant. Continuing in his grandfather's footsteps, Declan is the principal of Corofin's school. The farmhouse-style dinner is delicious and incorporates salad and vegetables from the large garden. The fire is lit in the little parlor and guests browse through the books and information on the area. Declan and Mary take great pride in their heritage and have compiled a booklet on the area, its history, and the points of interest. The little bedrooms (leave large cases in the car) all have a Gaelic names inscribed on a small plaque and are prettily decorated with pastel painted walls and flowered drapes and bedspreads. Beds are orthopedic and all but one of the rooms has a very tiny shower room (it has a large bathroom across the hall). Mary always puts a tiny posy, fruit and her information book in each room. For an extended stay the Kellehers have an attractive, self-catering cottage just down the road. The nearby Burren with its lunar-like landscape and distinctive flora, is most interesting, and the magnificent Cliffs of Moher are nearby. *Directions:* Shannon airport lies 37 kilometers to the south. From the airport take the N18 to Ennis, the N85 towards Lisdoonvarna, turn first right to Corofin, then, pass through the village, and the house is on your left after 1 kilometer.

FERGUS VIEW
Owners: Mary and Declan Kelleher
Kilnaboy
Corofin
Co Clare
tel: (065) 37606, fax: (065) 37192
6 rooms, 5 ensuite
From £16.50 per person B&B
Open April to September
Credit cards: none
B&B

Enniscoe House is owned and run by Susan Kellett, a descendant of the original family who settled this estate in the 1670s. This is the home of Susan and her son, and staying as her guest gives you a glimpse of what it was like to live in a grand country mansion—the old family furniture, portraits, books, and family memorabilia are yours to enjoy. The lofty rooms are decorated true to the Georgian period, and Susan works hard to see that everything is kept in tiptop condition. The three front bedrooms are of enormous proportions, reached by a grand elliptical staircase. Those in the older part of the house are small by comparison yet still most attractive. Dinners by soft, flickering candlelight are a real treat, with choices for each course, at little tables artfully arranged in the large dining room. Tucked behind the house and farmyard, dilapidated barns have received a new lease of life, with farm machinery and local artifacts on display, researchers assist those of Irish extraction in tracing their Mayo ancestors. Personable fishery manager Barry Segrave offers as much as or as little help as anglers need for fishing Lough Conn for brown trout and salmon (tel: 096 31853, fax: 096 31773). There are great cliffs along the north coast, where the Stone-Age settlements at Céide Fields are being excavated, and unspoilt areas of lakes, forests, and boglands around Nephin Mountain. *Directions:* From Ballina take the N59 to Crossmolina, turn left in town for Castlebar, and the house is on the left after 3 kilometers.

ENNISCOE HOUSE
Owner: Susan Kellett
Castlehill, Crossmolina
Co Mayo
tel: (096) 31112, fax: (096) 31773
6 rooms, 5 ensuite
From £44 per person B&B
Open April to mid-October
Credit cards: all major
Country house

Joe Moffatt was born at Kilmurray House, but after leaving school he had to emigrate to England. Joe always dreamed of his home in Ireland and many years later he returned with his young wife, Madge, to the farm. The house was in need of repair and their first thought was to build a modern bungalow nearby, but thankfully they realized the potential in Kilmurray House and persevered in its restoration. When their home was complete, Madge decided to open it to guests. The bedrooms are decorated in bright colors with coordinating bedspreads and walls—five have small rather dated shower rooms and the sixth a bathroom across the hall. The downstairs bedroom is suitable for people who have difficulty with stairs. The dining room tables are set with floral cloths and Madge discusses with her guests at breakfast what they would like to have for dinner—all the vegetables, fruit, beef, and lamb are from the farm. Joe is active in the local fishing club and enjoys planning outings for the avid fishermen who come to these parts to fish for brown trout and salmon. North Mayo is an interesting, though off-the-beaten-tourist-path area of Ireland. To the south lies Achill Island and to the north Yeats country. *Directions:* From Ballina go to Crossmolina, turn left in the town for Castlebar, pass the gates of Enniscoe House, and take the first turn to your right for the 3-kilometer drive to the farm.

KILMURRAY HOUSE
Owner: Madge and Joe Moffatt
Castlehill
Crossmolina
Co Mayo
tel: (096) 31227
6 rooms, 5 ensuite
From £15 per person B&B
Open March to October
Credit cards: none
Farmhouse B&B

Culdaff House has been in the Mills family since 1642, and until 1948, when George's mother decided to remove the front wing, it was a grand mansion. After the remodel, the furniture was sold, though a heavy sea chest (which reputedly came from a Spanish Armada vessel) and an enormous pine kitchen table remain, and Frances has added a couple of traditional pieces. Frances has done a tremendous job of making what could well have been a "white elephant" into a comfortable home and whatever shortcomings remain are more than made up for by her outgoing and friendly personality. Family bedrooms (there are five children) are interspersed with guestrooms, and guests have the use of two large bathrooms—one on each floor. Bedrooms, like all of the house, are prettily papered and simply furnished. There's a comfortable sitting room for relaxing round the fire, and with advanced notice Frances is happy to cook dinner, though guests usually walk into the village to eat. Culdaff has three very lively pubs where there's always plenty of entertainment. The Inishowen peninsula is very pretty with lots of ancient archaeological sites and quiet beaches. *Directions:* From Letterkenny take the N13 towards Derry to Bridgend where you turn north following signposts for Muff, Quigley's Point, Cardonagh, and Culdaff. Pass the village shops, bear left (beaches) and carry on straight into Culdaff House's driveway.

CULDAFF HOUSE   **NEW**
Owners: Frances and George Mills
Culdaff
Inishowen
Co Donegal
tel: (077) 79103
5 bedrooms sharing 2 bathrooms
From £15 per person B&B
Open March to December
Credit cards: none
Farmhouse B&B

Martinstown House was reputedly designed by Decimus Burton and built in the early 19th century as a shooting lodge for the 2nd Duke of Leinster. Tom Long is an accomplished horseman (though wife Meryl confines his collection of horsey memorabilia to their sitting room)—conversation often turns to things horsey, and hunting/riding can often be arranged. Garlands and swags decorate the upper walls in the tall-ceilinged drawing room and it is here or in the cozy little parlor that guest gather for drinks in the evening. Guests dine together, sometimes joined by Meryl and Tom. There are two bedrooms up the front staircase and two up the back. Front staircase rooms are larger and more sophisticated in their decor, each having a private bathroom just a few steps away across the hall. Up the narrow, winding, back staircase, two bedrooms share a bathroom: Meryl rents these rooms only to parties traveling together. Three race courses (The Curragh, Punchestown, and Naas) are nearby. The Irish National Stud and Japanese Gardens are 7 kilometers away and the Wicklow Mountains are an easy day trip. *Directions:* From Dublin take the Cork road (N7 which becomes the M7). Exit at Newbridge (before Kildare) and Curragh Camp is signposted (south) at the roundabout. Go through the army camp and straight at the Bramstan pub. Take the next left, right at the Bush pub and left at the next crossroads: the entrance to Martinstown is on your right.

MARTINSTOWN HOUSE **NEW**
Owners: Meryl and Tom Long
Curragh Camp
Co Kildare
tel: (045) 41269
4 rooms sharing 3 bathrooms
From £45 per person B&B
Closed Christmas
Credit cards: EC, MC, VS
Country house

Cleevaun has the advantage not only of an exquisite position facing the mouth of Dingle Bay, but also of being purposely built as a bed and breakfast, so each of the bedrooms has a modern ensuite shower or bathroom. The weather was blustery and cool when we stayed, but inside efficient central heating kept the house toasty and we appreciated the abundance of hot water in the shower and the luxury of towels hot from the heated towel rail. The decor is tasteful and uncluttered and several rooms have views across the fields to the bay. Guests are encouraged to come into the sitting room for a cup of tea and a slice of porter cake and to browse through an extensive collection of books and pamphlets on Ireland and the Dingle peninsula in particular, which will help you appreciate the beauty and folklore of the area. Pine tables and chairs are arranged to capture the lovely view of Dingle Bay from the adjacent dining room and guests enjoy a hearty breakfast before setting out to explore. It would be a pity to have come so far and not experience the peace and tranquillity which the unspoiled scenery of this area has to offer, so allow plenty of time for meandering down narrow country roads and walking along deserted beaches. The peninsula is rich in historical remains, particularly clochans or beehive huts which are believed to have been used as individual cells by ascetic monks in the earliest monasteries. *Directions:* Cleevaun is 2 kilometers beyond Dingle town on the road to Slea Head.

CLEEVAUN
Owners: Charlotte and Sean Cluskey
Lady's Cross
Dingle
Co Kerry
tel: (066) 51108, fax: (066) 51501 (attn.: Cleevaun)
9 ensuite rooms
From £16 per person B&B
Open March to November or on special request
Credit cards: EC, MC, VS
B&B

Doyle's Seafood Bar is famous the world over for excellent seafood. A small village shop and pub built in 1790 house the famous bar with its flagstone floor and cozy arrangements of tables and chairs. The acquisition of the house next door means that now John and Stella offer overnight accommodation as well as fine dining. The two houses are interconnected yet self-contained, so that guests can come and go to the bar and restaurant, but will not have their peace disturbed when they are sleeping. You step from the street into the old-fashioned parlor with its pine floor, grandfather clock, and sofas drawn into seating areas—large umbrellas are close at hand to aid you in bringing your luggage in, should the weather be inclement. The eight spacious guestrooms have ensuite bathrooms and are decorated in a comfortable, traditional style with 20th-century amenities such as television and phone. For complete privacy, opt for one of the four suites up the road which have their own private entrances. After dinner inquire at the bar, which of the many little pubs has traditional music that night and stroll along to join in the merriment. *Directions:* Dingle is a 2½-hour drive from Limerick. Turn right at the roundabout, right into John Street and Doyle's is on your left. Parking is on the street.

DOYLE'S SEAFOOD BAR & TOWNHOUSE
Owners: Stella and John Doyle
John Street
Dingle
Co Kerry
tel: (066) 51174, fax: (066) 51816
12 ensuite rooms
From £31 per person B&B
Open mid-March to mid-November
Credit cards: EC, MC, VS
Restaurant with rooms

Mary and John Curran built Greenmount House as a home for themselves and their small children, then expanded what was a moderately sized bungalow to make room for themselves and their bed-and-breakfast guests. A conservatory breakfast room, prettily furnished with painted pine furniture, takes advantage of a spectacular view across Dingle's rooftops to the harbor. Mary is especially proud of her breakfasts and tries to offer at least two fruit dishes as well as a cooked breakfast menu that includes cottage-cheese toastie and mushrooms in yogurt sauce as well as the traditional cooked breakfast. Breakfast is the only meal served and for dinner you can stroll down the hill into town where there are some particularly fine fish restaurants. If you relish the idea of choosing your lobster fresh from the tank, then go to Doyle's Seafood Bar. Guests enjoy a large living room, and tea and coffee fixings are always on hand in the little back dining room. Wander down to the harbor and watch the catch come in, window shop, and enjoy a pint in one of the many pubs. Explore the byways of the peninsula and if the weather is clement, take a trip to the Blasket Islands. The little village on the island is mostly in ruins and paths wander amongst fields where hardy islanders struggled until 1953 when the remaining residents were resettled on the mainland. *Directions:* Turn right at the roundabout in Dingle, next right into John Street and continue up the hill to Greenmount House.

GREENMOUNT HOUSE
Owners: Mary and John Curran
Gortonora
Dingle
Co Kerry
tel: (066) 51414, fax: (066) 51974
8 ensuite rooms
From £16 per person B&B
Open all year
Credit cards: none
B&B

Set on a wooded, tidal island in Donegal Bay and joined to the mainland by a narrow causeway, St Ernan's house was built in 1826 by John Hamilton, a nephew of the Duke of Wellington, for his wife. Over lunch here one day, Brian and Carmel O'Dowd decided that St Ernan's was the kind of hotel they would like to own, so several years later when it came on the market they took the plunge and forsook their careers in banking and teaching to become hoteliers. From almost every one of the rooms you are treated to marvelous views across a mirrorlike span of water. In the lounge, window seats offer views across the water to the mainland and chairs are artfully arranged to provide numerous nooks for intimate after-dinner conversation. A four-course candlelit dinner, with choices for each course, is served in the dining room. The attractive bedrooms come in all shapes and sizes, with the larger view rooms commanding the highest prices. Be sure to enjoy the walk around this delightful little island. The center of bustling Donegal town is The Diamond, a market place surrounded by shops (Magees sells the famous tweed), a hotel, and some pubs. Beyond Donegal town, lies the wild, rugged landscape that has made this county famous. *Directions:* From Sligo take the N15, towards Donegal and St Ernan's is signposted to your left 2 kilometers before you reach Donegal town.

ST ERNAN'S HOUSE HOTEL
Owners: Carmel and Brian O'Dowd
Donegal
Co Donegal
tel: (073) 21065, fax: (073) 22098
13 ensuite rooms
Double from £115
Open Easter to mid-November
Credit cards: EC, MC, VS
Country house hotel

Michael O'Brien and Marion Garry offer guests the friendliest of welcomes to Ariel House Rooms are available in a variety of price ranges from plain modern rooms that occupy a 1960's extension, to elegant Victorian bedrooms furnished with grand Victorian pieces. I particularly enjoyed our spacious room (222) with its tall, red velvet drapes, large sitting area, and stately mahogany furniture. All the rooms have television, telephone, and a hairdryer. Breakfast is the only meal served (either a Continental or full breakfast is available for an additional charge) and when not dining in the city, guests often walk a few yards down the road to eat in the conservatory at the Berkley Court Hotel or one of the several restaurants at the popular Jury's Hotel. There is off-the-road parking to the front and rear of the house. It is an easy walk to the 6, 7, and 8 bus routes and a three-minute ride on DART (Dublin Area Rapid Transit) to the rear of Trinity College. A 10% service charge is added to your bill and breakfast is not included in your tariff. *Directions:* Follow signs for the South City till you come to Baggot Street which continues south into Pembroke Street and Lansdowne Road (do not turn right in front of Jury's Hotel). Ariel House is on your left before you come to the Lansdowne Road Stadium.

ARIEL HOUSE
Owner: Michael O'Brien
Manager: Marion Garry
52 Lansdowne Road
Ballsbridge
Dublin 4
tel: (01) 6685512, fax: (01) 6685845
28 ensuite rooms
From £35 per person
Open all year
Credit cards: all major
Guesthouse

As you drive up the long avenue, Avondale House, just ten minutes from the heart of Dublin, appears more like a country farmhouse than a home. This is the relaxed and friendly home of Frank, a contemporary furniture designer, his wife, Josie, and their three sons, and they have decorated their home with great flair in an idiosyncratic style. A buoyant red sitting and dining room where contemporary pieces blend with Edwardian chairs and a lovely old circular dining table sets the tone. Across the hall, in the dramatic Gothic room, the soft flounces of vast quantities of muslin adorning the windows, contrast with the ecclesiastical carving of the bedhead, overmantle, and closet constructed from the ornately carved panels of an old organ case. White walls and tailored cream linen bedspreads and drapes provide a quiet background for the flamboyant black and red lacquer beds, chest, and closet in the Chinese room. Private bathrooms are just a few steps away down the hall. Adjoining Avondale House is a pitch and putt golf course. You can take walks along the canal and to Phoenix Park, that huge island of greenery in Dublin. *Directions:* From Dublin airport (a ten-minute drive) take the N1 (Dublin) to the N3, Navan road, and follow this road until Halfway House pub is on your right (also signposted Scribblestown Pitch and Putt). Turn right and follow this road across a junction to Avondale House on your right.

AVONDALE HOUSE   **NEW**
Owners: Josie and Frank Carroll
Scribblestown
Castleknock
Dublin 15
tel: (01) 8386545, fax: (01) 4539099
2 rooms with private bathrooms
£35 per person B&B
Closed mid-December to mid-January
Credit cards: none
Country house

Isolated by acres of fields and gardens, Belcamp Hutchinson is an oasis of country house elegance just fifteen minutes' drive from Dublin airport, making this the ideal first or last night's stop if you are flying to or from Dublin. However, it is such an outstanding home and Doreen is such a gracious hostess, that you will want to stay for several days. You'll doubtless be greeted by Buster, the German Shepherd, who brings along his toys in the hope that you'll be ready for a game. You'll know it's time for the drawing room fire to be lit when Clyde, the Rhodesian Ridgeback, wanders in. Up the elegant staircase, the bedrooms are decorated in strong, dark, Georgian colors, each beautifully coordinated with lovely fabrics. Burgundy can be a twin or a king room and has a sofa bed that can accommodate a child. Wedgwood has a romantic four-poster bed. Blue is a spacious double, while Terra cotta and Green are smaller rooms. Doreen always has three or four perfumes on the dresser and a variety of interesting magazines by the bedside. While the heart of Dublin is just a half hour's drive away, she also suggests that guests not overlook the opportunity to visit Newgrange, Malahide Castle, and the village of Howth. *Directions:* Belcamp Hutchinson is just off the Malahide Road in the Dublin suburb of Balgriffin.

BELCAMP HUTCHINSON   **NEW**
Owners: Doreen Gleson and Karl Waldburg
Carrs Lane
Malahide Road
Balgriffin
Dublin 17
tel: (01) 8460843, fax: (01) 8485703
5 ensuite rooms
From £36 per person B&B
Open all year
Credit cards: EC, MC, VS
Country house

Ballsbridge, just southeast of Dublin proper, is noted for its Victorian charm. Just across from the British Embassy, the pebbledash, Edwardian-style home of Mary and Gerard Doody offers twelve guestrooms in a three-story extension overlooking their grassy garden. Guests are given a front-door key and come and go through Mary and Gerard's home where they have a hallway seating area with a blazing fire and a comfortable sitting room. Breakfast is the only meal served, but there is no shortage of delightful restaurants and pubs within walking distance. Bedrooms are spacious and splendidly kitted out with phone, TV, and tea and coffee makings. Pastel-painted walls coordinate with attractive bedspreads and drapes and the rooms' uncluttered, tailored look is enhanced by fitted ash closets, bedheads, and bedside tables. While Merrion Road is a major thoroughfare, a quiet night's sleep is ensured by double-glazed windows. Two major attractions at the nearby Royal Dublin Society are the Agricultural Show in May and the Dublin Horse Show in August. A fifteen-minute bus ride brings you to the heart of Dublin. *Directions:* Follow signs for the South City to Baggot Street which becomes Pembroke Road. Turn right in front of Jury's Hotel into Merrion Road, continue past the Royal Dublin Society showgrounds, and Cedar Lodge is on your left opposite the British Embassy.

CEDAR LODGE   **NEW**
Owners: Mary and Gerard Doody
98 Merrion Road
Ballsbridge
Dublin 4
tel: (01) 6684410, fax: (01) 6684533
12 ensuite rooms
From £30 per person B&B
Open all year
Credit cards: EC, MC, VS
Guesthouse

The Hibernian Hotel, a grand, red-brick building, was constructed as a nurses' residence at the turn of the century and underwent a complete transformation to open as a lovely townhouse hotel in 1993. It is decorated throughout in a clubby, traditional style, with every piece of furniture new, so new in fact that this detracts from the old-world atmosphere the hotel is striving to create. Be that as it may, this is still the most charming hotel in Dublin with its library and drawing room full of luxuriously upholstered sofas and chairs arranged around fireplaces, and its sunny conservatory restaurant. The bedrooms are especially pleasing and equipped with everything from a full range of toiletries in the sparkling bathrooms to fax/modem point, hairdryer, TV, bowls of candies (licorice "allsorts"—my absolute favorite), and tea and coffee makings. The Hibernian Hotel is located on a quiet side street in the Victorian suburb of Ballsbridge, just a ten-minute stroll from St Stephen's Green, making it an ideal base for exploring the city. *Directions:* Follow signs for the South City. Cross the Baggot Street bridge into Baggot Street. Pass a row of shops on your left, turn left at the AIB bank, and the Hibernian Hotel is on your left. The hotel has a car park.

HIBERNIAN HOTEL **NEW**
Manager: David Butt
Eastmoreland Place
Upper Baggot Street
Ballsbridge
Dublin 4
tel: (01) 6687666, fax: (01) 6602655
29 ensuite rooms
Double from £135
Open all year
Credit cards: all major
City hotel

A tall, creeper-covered wall and a discreet plaque are the only indications that you have arrived at 31 Leeson Close. Ring the buzzer, open the tall doors, and you enter an oasis of tranquillity and greenery far from the clamor of the surrounding city. There are few fine examples of modern architecture in Ireland, and Number 31 must certainly rank amongst them. It was designed by and was home to Ireland's most controversial architect, Sam Stephenson. Now it is home to Mary and Brian Bennett who have kept the cool, clean lines of this modern home. A bright, contemporary painting hangs above the fireplace in the living room where the leather sofa, the only piece of furniture, hugs the wall of the conversation pit and stark, whitewashed brick walls contrast texturally with the mosaic tiled floor strewn with Oriental rugs. A glitzy mirrored bar is tucked in one corner. No two bedrooms are alike: the master bedroom has a skylight above the bed instead of a window, large bathroom with sauna, and his-and-her sinks, while another is long and skinny, rather like a railway carriage, with a patio, seating area, fitted beds going head to toe, and, a long, narrow bathroom. The upstairs bedroom is directly off the dining room. Breakfast is served anytime you want in the sunny, plant-filled conservatory. You can walk to everything and Mary encourages guests to come back during the day for rest and relaxation. *Directions:* Lower Leeson Street runs off the southern end of St Stephen's Green. Leeson Close is opposite 41 Lower Leeson Street.

NUMBER 31
Owners: Mary and Brian Bennett
31 Leeson Close
Dublin 2
tel: (01) 6765011, fax: (01) 6762929
5 ensuite rooms
From £29 per person B&B
Open all year
Credit cards: EC, MC, VS
B&B

It was during the 1860s that Dublin's residential areas were built and Ballsbridge emerged as a well-planned suburb of wide, tree-lined streets with fashionable redbrick houses fronted by impressive gardens. More recent times have seen this fashionable suburb come to house diplomatic missions and commercial institutions, but fortunately the aura of a sedate residential area has been retained. On one of Ballsbridge's most attractive streets, Raglan Lodge offers visitors a quiet respite from the hustle and bustle of the city. This splendid, three-story Victorian is Helen's home and she works very hard to keep everything in apple-pie order. The dining room doubles as a sitting room with groupings of little tables and chairs and a sofa set on its stripped pine floor. Breakfast is the only meal served and Helen has local restaurant menus on the hall table should guests decide to dine nearby. I particularly admired Room 1, a large ground-floor room with long, flowing drapes and tall ceilings with pretty cornices recalling the elegance of the Victorian era when this was a large private house. Just round the corner is the architecturally interesting American Embassy and Jury's Hotel with its many restaurants and popular cabaret show. A long walk or a short stroll and a bus ride will bring you into the heart of Dublin. *Directions:* Follow signs for the South City to Baggot Street which becomes Pembroke Street, turn right on Raglan Road and Raglan Lodge is on your left. There is plenty of off-the-road parking available should you be traveling with a car.

RAGLAN LODGE
Owner: Helen Moran
10 Raglan Road
Dublin 4
tel: (01) 6606697, fax: (01) 6606781
7 ensuite rooms
From £77
Closed Christmas
Credit cards: EC, MC, VS
Guesthouse

Just a few steps from St Stephen's Green, the Russell Court Hotel has a perfect location for exploring Dublin on foot. The hotel has grown like Topsy over the last few years and the ensuing contrast of styles and decor is rather jarring. However, I am continuing to include it in the pages of this guide because of its location and friendly staff, and in the hope that questions of design and decor will be resolved. Bedrooms are located up and down small staircases for this was once five separate townhouses (the tiny lift is suitable only for taking luggage to and from the rooms). All bedrooms are spacious and are decorated either in soft pinks and greens with light-wood furniture in an art deco-ish style or in dark maroons and blues with dark-wood, traditional furniture. At the time of my visit all rooms had the same price, making rooms like 111 with its bed and a circular dais, 112 with its four-poster bed, and 300, a paneled attic room with separate living room and bedroom, surprisingly good value for money. While there is a small traditional restaurant, guests often enjoy a barbecue in the beer garden (May to September) or a more casual meal in Dicey Riley's. Set up like an old-fashioned Irish shop, bar, and barn, this large room is decorated with an eclectic mixture of Irish bygones and is a lively place to visit in the evening when business people socialize before going home from work. A 12½% service charge is added to your bill. *Directions:* Take Harcourt Street from the southwestern corner of St Stephen's Green and Russell Court Hotel is on your right. The hotel has off the road parking.

RUSSELL COURT HOTEL
Managers: John Killeen and Michael Flanagan
21-25 Harcourt Street
Dublin 2
tel: (01) 6784066, fax: (01) 6781576
42 ensuite rooms
Double from £80
Open all year
Credit cards: all major
City hotel

Irish nobility and country gentlemen needed to spend time in Dublin, so in 1824 the Shelbourne opened its doors to the gentry who did not have a residence in the city. Since day one, the Shelbourne has been "the" place to stay and today it remains as Dublin's deluxe hotel, suffused with the elegance of other eras, living up to its motto as "the most distinguished address in Ireland." The comings and goings of Dublin are reflected in the enormous gilt mirrors of the Lord Mayor's Lounge where people gather to enjoy a sophisticated afternoon tea. Traditional decor, good conversation, and the presence of Dublin characters combine to make the Horseshoe Bar a most convivial place. The very elegant dining room provides equally elegant food, while the adjacent Shelbourne Bar provides a less sophisticated, clubby dining alternative and the opportunity to enjoy a convivial drink. Everything is delightful in the bedrooms (48 smaller rooms comprise The Executive Wing, which are allocated primarily to business clients and one night stays) and a premium is charged for those with views of St Stephens Green. There are twenty-two opulent suites. This landmark historic hotel overlooks St Stephen's Green, a refreshing oasis of greenery in the center of this bustling city. A 15% service charge is added to your bill. Breakfast is not included in the tariff. *Directions:* The Shelbourne Hotel is on the north side of St Stephen's Green. Park in front of the hotel and the porter will take care of your car.

SHELBOURNE HOTEL
Manager: Donal O'Gallagher
St Stephen's Green
Dublin 2
tel: (01) 6766471, fax: (01) 6616006
164 ensuite rooms
Double from £150
Open all year
Credit cards: all major
City hotel

Norah Brown so loves to cook that she not only provides dinners for her guests, but on weekends she opens up her dining room to non-residents looking for a special meal. Norah uses fresh local ingredients and a great deal of culinary skill to create an exquisite evening repast. Ralph discusses the menu over drinks in the den and both he and Norah join their guests for coffee and conversation in the drawing room. Norah is an inveterate collector, filling every nook and cranny with collections of old china, pewter, stoneware and fascinating bygones. Upstairs are the very comfortable, attractively decorated bedrooms, one of which has its own bathroom downstairs. If you are intensely interested in the production or are an avid collector of crystal, you can tour the nearby Tyrone Crystal factory and see firsthand the hand-blowing and cutting of sparkling crystal. The National Trust has two properties close at hand: Ardress House, a 17th-century manor and The Argory, an 1820s house with a lot of original furniture set in 300 acres of woodland. A half-hour drive brings you to the Ulster American Folk Park, a collection of historic cottages and buildings that tells the story of the great migrations of Ulster people to the New World. *Directions:* Take the M1 from Belfast to junction 15 where you take the A29 towards Armagh for 2 kilometers to the left-hand turn to Grange. Turn immediately right and Grange Lodge is the first house on the right.

GRANGE LODGE
Owners: Norah and Ralph Brown
Grange Road
Dungannon
Co Tyrone
tel: (018687) 84212, fax: (018687) 23891
4 rooms, 3 ensuite
From £27.50 per person B&B
Open all year
Credit cards: EC, MC, VS
Country house

The summertime evening view from the dining room is simply staggering. As the night slowly draws in on green fields that tumble to the sea and scudding clouds dapple the reddening sky, the sun slowly sinks behind the distant Slieve League, the highest sea cliffs in Europe. The food is as spectacular as the view and served in such portions that satisfy even the heartiest of Irish appetites. Thierry Delcros and his dynamic young wife, Claire, took the plunge and converted what was a nondescript farmhouse with a spectacular view into a restaurant with rooms. Thierry has cooked at various hotels and restaurants in Ireland for some years now and earned quite a reputation for fine French cooking tailored to the Irish palate. The price of a meal is very reasonable, based on the cost of the main course, and there is an emphasis on fresh local seafood. Perhaps the best way to secure an often hard-to-come-by dinner reservation is to stay here, so that after an evening-long repast you can retire up the narrow pine staircase to one of the smart, tailored bedrooms with their tweedy carpet and matching drapes and bedspreads. If you are lucky, you will be able to secure one that captures the view across the bay. Between breakfast and dinner the rugged Donegal landscape is yours to explore—be sure to include a visit to Glencolumbkille Folk Village. *Directions:* From Donegal take the N56 towards Killybegs. The left-hand turn to Castle Murray House is in Dunkineely.

CASTLE MURRAY HOUSE
Owners: Claire and Thierry Delcros
Dunkineely
Co Donegal
tel: (073) 37022/37330
10 ensuite rooms
From £22 per person B&B
Closed February
Restaurant closed Mondays except in summer
Credit cards: all major
Restaurant with rooms

This dazzling, three-story Regency house, formerly the dower house of the Courtown estate, has an atmosphere of refined elegance created by your vivacious hostess, Mary Bowe. Mary has great charm and energy—during our stay she chatted with guests before dinner, made the rounds during dinner, and was back again at breakfast checking up to make certain that everything was perfect. The house is full of antiques, classic pieces that transport you back to the days of gracious living in grand houses. While we especially enjoyed our large, twin-bedded room with impressive, well-polished furniture, elegant decor, and a grand bathroom, I found the other bedrooms equally attractive. Six prized units are the ultra-luxurious gorgeously decorated State Rooms tucked away in a separate ground-floor wing; request the Print Suite, Stopford, Georgian, or French. Dinner is served in the ornate Victorian Gothic conservatory dining room—all greenery and mirrors. The food is a delight—superb French and Irish dishes. This is one of the few hotels in Ireland where it is appropriate to dress for dinner. An atmosphere of formal extravagance prevails: it is very much Mary Bowe's personal vision of a country house hotel, quite unsuitable for children. A 10% service charge is added to your bill. *Directions:* Marfield House is 88 kilometers from Dublin. Take the N11 south to Gorey and as you enter the town turn left, before going under the railway bridge, onto the Courtown Road: the house is on your right after 2 kilometers.

MARFIELD HOUSE
Owner: Mary Bowe
Courtown Road
Gorey
Co Wexford
tel: (055) 21124
19 ensuite rooms,
Double from £150
Closed December and January
Credit cards: all major
Country house hotel

If you enjoy horse-riding, Tillman and Collette Anhold offer the experienced rider week-long riding vacations at their farm. It has the most magnificent position overlooking vast stretches of empty golden beaches and little green islands, while at its back rise the rugged Ben Bulben Mountains. On arrival Collette sees that you are settled into one of the snug, pine-paneled bedrooms, then it's off to the stables to meet your fine Irish hunter. Your four-legged friend is yours to ride just when and where you want to—along unspoiled beaches, through green mountain forests, and along a cross-country course jumping walls and wooden fences. You are expected to look after him by feeding, grooming, and tacking up. Collette provides a hearty breakfast and a full four-course dinner, serving it to guests seated around the large dining-room table. A spirit of happy camaraderie prevails as guests gather in the evening around the fire in the large stone fireplace to have horsy conversations. If you wish to range farther afield, Tillman can also arrange seven-day treks on the Sligo Trail and fourteen-day treks on the Donegal Trail where overnight accommodation is provided in traditional farmhouses. As you will not need a car for your holiday, it is suggested that you take the train to Sligo where a transfer will be organized. *Directions:* Grange is north of Sligo on the road to Donegal. Horse Holiday Farm is on your left.

HORSE HOLIDAY FARM
Owners: Collette and Tillman Anhold
Grange
Co Sligo
tel: (071) 66152 fax: (071) 66400
6 ensuite rooms
From £600 per person per week
Dinner, B&B, and horse
Open Easter to November
Credit cards: none
B&B and stables

Temple, which is almost at the geographic center of Ireland, was home to Declan's grandparents who were farmers hereabouts. While Declan still keeps a small herd of sheep, he and Bernadette concentrate more on tourism, offering cycling and walking holidays and relaxation weekends with classes in yoga, massage, aromatherapy, and shiatsu. A fire is lit in the cosy parlor in the evening and it is here that guests relax after dinner 'round the long dining room table where they often dine on lamb from the farm and vegetables and fruit from the huge organic vegetable garden. Bedrooms are delightful: one fresh and flowery with a brass and wrought-iron bed, another enormous, home to a grand, draped, metal and brass bed, and the Bishops room all dark polished wood—the room was built for an elderly bishop who retired to live with his relatives. Downstairs is a family room with a separate child's room colorfully decorated in a gay nursery print. Guests can borrow bikes and Bernadette has lots of tourist information on this often-neglected part of Ireland. The bog train, a small train that chugs you through a vast bogland while a guide explains its history and management is popular with guests. Just down the road in Killbeggan are Locke's whiskey distillery while the Clonmacnois monastic ruins and round tower overlooking the River Shannon are a half-hour's drive away. *Directions:* Temple is about a kilometer off the N6 midway between Dublin and Galway, between Horseleap and Moate. The house is very well signposted.

TEMPLE
Owners: Bernadette and Declan Fagan
Horseleap
Moate
Co Westmeath
tel: (0506) 35118 fax: (0506) 35118
4 ensuite rooms
From £20 per person B&B
Open March to November
Credit cards: EC, MC, VS
Farmhouse B&B

The Irish name for Kenmare, *An Neidin*, means "the little nest," which is a good description of this attractive town nestling beside the Kenmare river at the foot of some of Ireland's most spectacular scenery. Kenmare's two main roads are wide and spacious, lined with bustling shops. On a quieter side street, Hawthorne House offers visitors an attractive guesthouse just a few steps from the town's main street. Inside, the old house has received a complete facelift with light pine replacing all the old woodwork and doors, the decor borders on fussy and they are rather overfond of heavily scented potpourri. The bedrooms, all named after districts around Kenmare, are decorated in a flowery, contemporary style. Derrynid, Neidin, and Dromore are superior rooms (well worth the extra cost), having the additional facilities of a spacious sitting area, color television, hairdryer, bottled spring water and flowers. Standard rooms are small and it is advisable to leave large suitcases in the car. The dining room, all decked out in shades of pink, offers a set evening meal if you do not want to eat at one of the several restaurants in Kenmare. Guests often drive around the Ring of Kerry, competing with coaches for views and vistas that are much overrated. Rides to Bantry and Killarney provide stunning vistas. *Directions:* Kenmare is about a three-hour drive from Shannon on the N71 between Killarney and Bantry. Hawthorne House is adjacent to the Park Hotel. A large car park provides safe, off-the-road parking.

HAWTHORNE HOUSE
Owners: Trina and Kevin Murphy
Shelbourne Street
Kenmare
Co Kerry
tel: (064) 41035
8 rooms, 7 ensuite
From £23 per person B&B
Closed February
Credit cards: EC, MC, VS
Guesthouse

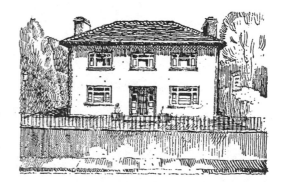

The Park Hotel began life in 1897 as the Great Southern Hotel Kenmare to provide a convenient overnight stop for railway travelers en route to or from the Ring of Kerry. The furnishings are those of a hotel of the late Victorian or Edwardian age—almost every piece of furniture is antique, some of it massive, but somehow in keeping and much of it very valuable. Francis Brennan came here to manage and stayed to own. He has charm, humor, and professionalism, all of which have infected his young staff. Guests are greeted by a blazing coal fire which casts its glow towards the cozy bar and lounge, and you sit down at a partners' desk to register before being shown to your room. Such touches give a small-hotel feeling to this large hotel. Exquisite accommodations are provided in nine very luxurious and very pricey suites with splendid views out over the Kenmare Bay. Bedrooms in the main hotel are large and pleasant, those in the newer wing uniform in size, all with big-city prices. The cooking is excellent and has been awarded a Michelin star. The menu offers some tempting choices and the cellars offer a fine selection of wines. The Park Hotel provides programs for the Christmas and New Year holidays. Adjacent to the hotel is an eighteen-hole golf course and the hotel also arranges golfing programs at Killarney, Ballybunion, and Waterville. Fishing programs can be arranged. *Directions:* Kenmare is about a three-hour drive from Shannon on the N71 between Killarney and Bantry.

PARK HOTEL
Owner: Francis Brennan
Kenmare
Co Kerry
tel: (064) 41200, fax: (064) 41402
40 ensuite rooms
Double from £196
Open April to Christmas
Credit cards: all major
Luxury resort

Kenmare is one of my favorite Irish towns, and how appropriate that one of my favorite B&Bs, Sallyport House, is located here. Janie Arthur returned home after working for fifteen years in California to help her brother, John, convert the family home into luxurious guest accommodation, decorating it in an uncluttered, sophisticated style. Return in the evening to chat round the fire in the drawing room or curl up in one of the comfortable chairs in the less formal sitting area with its exposed stone wall and photographs of Kenmare at the turn of the century. Breakfast is the only meal served. For dinner, it's a two-minute walk into town. The bedrooms are delightful, each furnished with antiques and accompanied by a large luxurious bathroom. Muxnaw has views of Muxnaw mountain and deep window seats; Ring View looks out to the Kenmare River; Reen a Gross has an American king-sized four-poster bed; The Falls has a view of the pretty garden. It's delightful to stroll along the riverbank, through the park, and back through the town. You can spend several days exploring the Beara peninsula, Ring of Kerry and Lakes of Killarney *Directions:* Kenmare is about a three-hour drive from Shannon on the N71 between Killarney and Bantry. From Bantry, Sallyport House is on your right just after you cross the bridge. From Killarney follow Bantry signposts through Kenmare and Sallyport House is on your left before you come to the bridge.

SALLYPORT HOUSE　　**NEW**
Owners: Janie and John Arthur
Kenmare
Co Kerry
tel: (064) 42066 fax: (064) 41752
5 ensuite rooms
From £25 per person B&B
Open Easter to mid-November
Credit cards: none
B&B

Apparently Dunromin's former owner was an insurance agent who had traveled all over Ireland, so when he bought this house he changed its name from Whittington Cottage to reflect his circumstances, "done roaming." A narrow strip of garden separates the house from the busy main road so there's lots of traffic noise, but Dunromin is one of the few listings in this book that is within easy walking distance of bus and rail transportation. Guests have a snug sitting room where Valerie provides a carefully compiled book detailing the many attractions of the town and leaflets for guests to take. Valerie discusses the merits of the various restaurants and pubs and has sample menus on hand. Traditional Irish music is a feature of the local pubs, but as it does not start until very late in the evening, guests often ask Tom for a couple of tunes on his accordion and he is always happy to oblige. Upstairs Tom has done an excellent job of fitting small shower rooms into the bedrooms and Valerie has made the little rooms very pretty with attractive wallpaper, drapes, and bedcovers. A ten-minute walk brings you to the picturesque heart of this lovely town with its many fine old buildings, including beautifully painted shops and pubs with hand-crafted signs. Kilkenny Castle is definitely worth a visit. *Directions:* From Carlow take the N10 to Kilkenny. At the first roundabout follow signs for the city center and you will find Dunromin on your right after 1 kilometer.

DUNROMIN   **NEW**
Owners: Valerie and Tom Rothwell
Dublin Road
Kilkenny
Co Kilkenny
tel: (056) 61387
4 ensuite rooms
From £14 per person B&B
Open all year
Credit cards: VS, MC
B&B

There are a wealth of bed and breakfasts in Killarney and I have selected Beaufield House not only for its location and pleasing decor, but also because it is run most professionally by Danny Bowe who was for many years the manager of nearby Ryan's Hotel. Danny and his wife, Moya, decided they wanted to work for themselves and Beaufield House, a purpose built bed and breakfast, is the result. Eight bedrooms have a twin as well as a double bed, making them ideal for families or friends traveling together, and all the rooms are neat and modern, decorated with pale colors. All have television and shower rooms. There is a comfortable sitting room with tourist information and television. A hearty breakfast is the only meal served, but there are restaurants to suit every pocket, in the town. Killarney is a tourist town, thronged with visitors in the busy summer months. On the outskirts of town is Muckross House, a Tudor-style house on the shores of the Killarney lakes. Here you can hire a pony and trap, not an inexpensive proposition, tour the house, furnished in Victorian style, watch artisans practice their skills in the old farm buildings, and visit the tea room. *Directions:* Keep on the N22 Limerick to Cork road avoiding the busy town center and turn right in front of Ryan's Hotel—this is Cork Road and Beaufield House is on your left.

BEAUFIELD HOUSE
Owners: Moya and Danny Bowe
Cork Road
Killarney
Co Kerry
tel: (064) 34440 fax: (064) 34663
15 ensuite rooms
From £18 per person B&B
Open all year
Credit cards: all major
Guesthouse

The Cahernane Hotel, built in 1877, was once the grand home of the Herbert family who were the Earls of Pembroke. As a result of their lavish lifestyle, the Herberts went into bankruptcy and it is only in recent years that the house has been restored and renovated to its former glory. Pine and blond oak woodwork, over the years worn to a lovely patina, gives an old-world feeling to the elegant old house. A blazing log fire and deep sofas in the spacious entrance hall beckon a country-house welcome. Up the grand staircase are several comfortable, old-fashioned bedrooms offering superb views of the surrounding estate through their tall windows (rooms in the attic are not recommended). As a direct contrast to this mellow scene, a wing of modern bedrooms has been added to one side of the house, bridged by a large glass sun-lounge. Here the bright white rooms have black wooden furniture and contemporary fabric drapes and bedspreads that blends well with the bright purple carpet. This is a large hotel by this guide's standard and it has a relatively impersonal hotel-like atmosphere. *Directions:* The Cahernane Hotel is 2 kilometers from the center of Killarney on the N71, Kenmare road.

CAHERNANE HOTEL
Manager: Conor O'Connell
Killarney
Co Kerry
tel: (064) 31895 fax: (064) 34340
45 ensuite rooms
Double from £120
Open Easter to November
Credit cards: all major
Country house hotel

Kathleen O'Regan-Sheppard possesses boundless energy, taking great pride in keeping her house in tiptop condition, planning improvements (heated cupboards for golfers to dry their bags and boots are her latest innovation), working with the hotel keepers association, and being a wife and mother. Kathleen is especially proud of her collection of contemporary watercolors by local artists. Guests enjoy the large lobby parlor, often gathering here with friends after dinner. The bedrooms are of the highest standards with orthopedic beds, tea-and coffee-makings, telephone, hairdryer, and color television. Those in the newer wing enjoy especially large bright bathrooms. A hearty breakfast is the only meal served. Recommendations are made for nearby restaurants for dinner. A measure of Kathleen's success is that over 50% of her guests are repeat visitors. Whether viewed from a boat or a pony and trap, the lakes of Killarney are beautiful but in summer the town is very crowded. Enjoy Muckross House and Ross Castle but be sure to allow time (on a fine day) to drive through the Gap of Dunloe. *Directions:* Kathleen's Country House is situated in the countryside a 3-kilometer drive from Killarney on the N22, Tralee road.

KATHLEEN'S COUNTRY HOUSE
Owner: Kathleen O'Regan-Sheppard
Tralee Road
Killarney
Co Kerry
tel: (064) 32810 fax: (064) 32340
16 ensuite rooms
From £32 per person B&B
Open March to November and Christmas
Credit cards: EC, MC, VS
Guesthouse

This traditional farmhouse in the rich farmlands of County Cork, is run by Margaret Browne who was voted Ireland's "Housewife of the Year 1990." Margaret started doing bed and breakfast in a small way when her children were young. Now it is a most professional operation and she has had the house altered to incorporate her growing endeavors: all the bedrooms have smart, ensuite bathrooms, the dining room has been extended so that non-guests can come for a special meal, and a sunny conservatory and hard tennis court have been built for guests' enjoyment. Yet this remains very much a working farm where you wander across the garden to explore the farmyard and watch the cows being milked. There is a particularly pretty sitting room all decked out in shades of green with Victorian sofas. Bedrooms are named after local rivers and all are attractively decorated with well-chosen antique furniture, wallpaper, and fabrics. The same care goes into the care and feeding of her guests—Margaret uses only the finest local meats, fish, and vegetables. The nearby fishing port of Youghal (pronounced yawl) is famous for its delightful old buildings and having had Sir Walter Raleigh as its mayor. You can take a walking tour of the town's medieval streets. The Midleton Jamestown Heritage Center tells the history of Irish whiskey production. Cobh (pronounced cove) has an interesting maritime museum. *Directions:* Killeagh is on the N25 between Youghal and Cork. Turn at The Old Thatch Tavern, then after 1 kilometer turn right: Ballymakeigh House is on your right after 1 kilometer.

BALLYMAKEIGH HOUSE
Owners: Margaret and Michael Browne
Killeagh
Co Cork
tel: (024) 95184 fax: (024) 95184
5 ensuite rooms
From £20 per person B&B
Open all year
Credit cards: none
Farmhouse B&B

Flemingstown House, an 18th-century farmhouse, is just an hour's drive south of Limerick and Shannon airport, a quiet countryside world away from the hustle and bustle of the cosmopolitan area. Walk round the farm, watch the cows being milked, and chat with Imelda as she works in her spacious kitchen—for the two things that Imelda loves are cooking and taking care of her guests. It would be a shame to stay and not eat, for Imelda prepares tempting meals in which, following the starter and soup, there is a choice of meat or fish as a main course and always three or four desserts and farm cheeses made by her sister and her husband. The intricate stained-glass windows of the conservatory-style dining room were made by the same artist as those in the local church. Upstairs, the low ceilinged bedrooms are snug in size, and come with a variety of twin and double combinations that can accommodate families of all sizes. The decor is simple and attractive, with painted walls and matching bedcovers and drapes, and each room has a small shower room. Nearby Kilmallock has the ruins of two friaries and the remains of its fortified wall weaving through the town. Imelda's guests often use her home as a base for touring counties Limerick, Tipperary, Kerry, and Cork. *Directions:* From Limerick take the N20 (Cork road) for 40 kilometers and turn left to Kilmallock (10 kilometers). From Kilmallock take the Kilfinane road (R512) for 3 kilometers and the house is on your left.

FLEMINGSTOWN HOUSE **NEW**
Owner: Imelda Sheedy-King
Kilmallock
Co Limerick
tel: (063) 98093 fax: (063) 98546
6 rooms, 5 ensuite
From £15 per person B&B
Closed December
Credit cards: none
Farmhouse B&B

After leaving Clifden you bounce along seemingly endless kilometers of single-track road, but persevere for it is well worth all the effort you put into getting to Kille House as it is one of the most attractive B&Bs. Anya and Jan Voormolen came here on holiday from Holland, fell in love with the wild beauty of Connemara, bought Kille House in a sad state of neglect, and have done a fantastic job of restoring and refurbishing this sturdy house. Beyond the sheltered confines of the garden, you are treated to fabulous vistas of rocky fields tumbling to the distant bay with a backdrop of rugged mountains. Unfortunately Anya was out when I visited, but happily a carpenter was hard at work and he escorted me round the handsome rooms, each beautifully decorated in a country-house style and filled with lovely antiques. Breakfast and dinner can be taken in the dining room or in the large country kitchen. There's a lot to do in the area: you can take a day trip from Cleggan to Inishbofin Island; from Clifden you can follow the lovely coast road through Ballyconneely and Roundstone while nearby Connemara National Park offers fabulous walks and an interpretive center. *Directions:* Take the N59 from Galway to Clifden and follow the one-way system to the top of the town where you take the Sky Road (high road at the 'Y' both here and when you are on the headland) for 9 kilometers of single-track road. After you round the headland, Kille House is signposted to your left.

KILLE HOUSE **NEW**
Owners: Anya and Jan Voormolen
Kingstown
Clifden
Co Galway
tel: (095) 21849 fax: (095) 21849
4 rooms, 2 ensuite
From £20 per person B&B
Open March to November
Credit cards: none
B&B

Michael and Marie used to own The Vintage restaurant. Patrons were always asking them for advice on where to stay, so when the Munster and Leinster Bank closed its doors, they saw an opportunity to purchase this tall townhouse to provide them with accommodation they could wholeheartedly recommend. Since selling their restaurant Michael and Marie have devoted their energies to the Old Bank House—Michael cooks breakfast and Marie is often on hand to greet guests. Bedrooms are spick-and-span and tastefully decorated. Each has a phone and TV and all except the family room have bathrooms with showers over the tub. Rooms at the front enjoy distant harbor views and if you want "the" view, request Room 9, an attic room, but bear in mind that this is a tall, skinny house and there are a lot of stairs to climb to your aerie (it's the honeymoon suite and the most expensive room in the house). Breakfast is served by young, uniformed staff in the dining room. The location at the very heart of this most attractive harbor town is ideal: you can stroll round the shops perusing the restaurant menus as you go (Kinsale has a much-vaunted reputation as the gourmet dining capital of Ireland), or take time out from food for a bracing walk along the yacht-filled harbor or along the cliffs of the Old Head of Kinsale. *Directions:* Follow the main road into Kinsale (Pearse Street) and you will find the Old Bank House on the right. Parking is on the street.

OLD BANK HOUSE
Owners: Marie and Michael Riese
Pearse Street
Kinsale
Co Cork
tel: (021) 774075
9 ensuite rooms
From £35 per person B&B
Open all year
Credit cards: all major
B&B

You find The Old Presbytery amongst the narrow, tile-hung houses that terrace up from Kinsale's yacht-filled harbor. Cathleen and Ken Buggy are inveterate collectors of country-style bygones and every nook and cranny is filled with their treasures. The effect is quaint and country-cozy. The dining room, hung with gleaming copper pans and warmed by a blackened, wood-burning stove, is the old kitchen. Ken loves to cook and sometimes in the summer he offers a dinner based on fresh fish in addition to a delectable breakfast that includes fresh-baked soda bread, homemade yogurt, and freshly squeezed orange juice as well as the traditional Irish breakfast. Ken tempts his guests out of bed in the morning by wafting the aroma of fresh coffee and baking bread up the stairs. Up the narrow stairs, linen sheets grace Victorian brass beds in rooms filled with country memorabilia. This is altogether an exceptionally attractive house. Please remember this is a small house with lots of furniture—leave large suitcases in the car. *Directions:* Go straight up the main street in Kinsale (Pearse Street) to the end, turn left, first right, and first right, and The Old Presbytery is the first house on the right. The Old Presbytery has a large enclosed yard for off-road parking.

THE OLD PRESBYTERY
Owners: Cathleen and Ken Buggy
43 Cork Street
Kinsale
Co Cork
tel: (021) 772027
6 rooms, 5 ensuite
From £20 per person B&B
Closed Christmas
Credit cards: none
B&B

In the north corner of Kinsale harbor is a wooded promontory on which there is a village within the town called Scilly. Here, commanding the most idyllic views of the yacht-speckled harbor, Charles Fort, and the encircling green hills is Scilly House Inn, the home of Karin Young and Bill Skelly. Karin hails from California and Bill from Ireland and, loving both places, they divide their time between the two. Decorated in an uncluttered, luxurious style, their home makes the most of the views across the lawns and gardens down to the water. From the ground-floor garden room with its shaded balcony overlooking the harbor to the luxurious suite with its glassed-in porch capturing glorious views, the bedrooms are a delight (one bedroom does not have a view, and another is tucked in an adjacent cottage), decorated in an uncluttered, sophisticated style. Breakfasts are another treat with fresh fruit, scrambled eggs with smoked salmon, and fluffy omelets on the menu. Dinner is available for parties of more than six people. The adjacent pub, The Spaniard, with its low-beamed bars and stone-flagged floors is worth a visit. Walk along the harbor shore into Kinsale or set your sights on Charles Fort where William Penn's father once worked as governor of Kinsale. *Directions:* Follow the road that fronts the harbor to the east which brings you into the district of Kinsale known as Scilly and Scilly House is on your right.

SCILLY HOUSE INN
Owners: Karin Young and Bill Skelly
Scilly
Kinsale
Co Cork
tel: (021) 772413 fax: (021) 774629
7 ensuite rooms
From £40 per person B&B
Open mid-April to November
Credit cards: all major
Country house

As the name implies, Laragh Trekking Centre specializes in trekking through the surrounding mountains high atop a magnificent Shire or Clydesdale horse. David leads guests on treks that vary in length from one hour (for the inexperienced) to all day (for the experienced) along forestry paths and across the mountain, returning to a tail-wagging welcome from Winston, the labrador. John and Noreen's home is a rather architecturally uninteresting bungalow which in contrast, offers the most magnificent view of forest, distant mountains, and waterfalls from its sitting room. Noreen takes great pride in her bedrooms with their matching spreads and drapes and coordinating towels and sheets. While the rooms have everything— direct dial telephone, TV, tea and coffee makings, and lots of toiletries—Noreen says that she gets more compliments on the excellence of her showers than on any other feature. A little gift shop sells postcards and gifts, and in amongst the leprechauns and postcards, I spotted some very pretty Celtic rings and tapes of traditional Irish music. Guests enjoy feeding the horses, walking the forestry trails, and visiting the nearby famous monastic city of Glendalough. *Directions*: From Dublin take the N11 to Kilmacanogue where you turn right for Glendalough. Eight kilometers after Roundwood, as you enter Laragh, bear right and Laragh Trekking Centre is on your right after 2 kilometers.

LARAGH TREKKING CENTRE   **NEW**
Owners: Noreen and David McCallow
Laragh East
Glendalough
Co Wicklow
tel: (0404) 45282 fax: (0404) 45204
6 rooms, 5 ensuite
From £16 per person B&B
Open all year
Credit cards: EC, MC, VS
B&B with stables

When the British built this army complex in 1800, they could never have imagined that it would serve for many years as the village school and more recently become a delightful restaurant that, fortunately for the traveler, offers accommodation. Pine tables and chairs and a massive dresser filled with pretty pottery give the restaurant a country air which extends up the steep pine staircase to the attractive little bedrooms set under the steeply sloping roof. All the bedrooms have an antique pine dresser or table, and a tea and coffee tray. You order your breakfast the night before so that it is ready for you at the time of your choosing. Breakfast service ends at 10 am and last orders for dinner are 9 pm, but beyond that there is a great deal of flexibility about when lunch, afternoon tea, and dinner are served. I arrived at 5 pm on a Sunday and the restaurant was crowded with patrons enjoying a very late lunch, afternoon tea, and an early dinner. A large sign on the front of the building states that Mitchells does not cater for children—best be forewarned. The remains of the monastic city of Glendalough with its round tower and seven churches is just down the road and there are spectacular gardens and houses to visit nearby. *Directions:* From Dublin take the N11 to Kilmacanogue where you turn right for Glendalough. Eight kilometers after Roundwood, as you enter Laragh, bear right to Mitchells.

MITCHELLS OF LARAGH   **NEW**
Owners: Margaret and Jerry Mitchell
The Old Schoolhouse
Laragh
Glendalough
Co Wicklow
tel: (0404) 45302 fax: (0404) 45302
5 ensuite rooms
From £19 per person B&B
Open all year
Credit cards: all major
Restaurant with rooms

Delphi Lodge with its surrounding estate, was for centuries the sporting estate of the Marquis of Sligo. This wild, unspoilt, and beautiful valley with its towering mountains, tumbling rivers, and crystal-clear loughs was acquired in 1986 by Peter and Jane Mantle. Fortunately for those who have a love of wild, beautiful places, they have restored the Marquis's fishing lodge and opened their home to guests who come to walk, fish for salmon, relax, and enjoy the camaraderie of the house-party atmosphere. In the evening Peter presides at the head of the very long dinner table (when a guest catches a salmon they take the place of honor) and guests enjoy a leisurely meal and conversation, of all things fishing. A snug library and an attractive drawing room are at hand and guests often spend late night hours in the billiards room. Bedrooms are all furnished in contemporary pine, several having large comfortable armchairs and views to the peaceful lake. Such is the popularity of the place that it is advisable to make reservations well in advance to secure a summer booking. Four deluxe, self-catering cottages are also available on the estate. *Directions:* Leenane is between Wesport and Clifden on the N59. From Leenane go north towards Westport for 5 kilometers, turn left and continue along the north shore of Killary harbor towards Louisburgh for 10 kilometers. Delphi Lodge is in the woods, on the left after the adventure center.

DELPHI LODGE
Owners: Jane and Peter Mantle
Leenane
Co Galway
tel: (095) 42211 fax: (095) 42296
7 ensuite rooms
From £35 per person B&B
Open February to October
Credit cards: EC, MC, VS
Country house

Rosleague Manor is a lovely Irish hotel—a comfortable, country-house hotel overlooking Ballinakill Bay and an ever-changing panorama of wild Connemara countryside. This is a quiet, sparsely populated land of steep hills, tranquil lakes, and grazing sheep, where narrow country lanes lead to little hamlets. Owner Anne Foyle is much in evidence making certain that guests are well taken care of. The hotel is beautifully furnished with lovely old furniture; the lounges are cozy with their turf fires and comfortable chairs. The garden-style conservatory is a popular place for before or after-dinner drinks. Bedrooms are decorated to the highest of standards—request a ground floor room if you have difficulty with stairs. The five-course dinner is from a fixed price menu with four or five choices for each course. Dishes vary with the seasons and include a wide selection of locally caught fish and Connemara lamb. This is a peaceful place to hide away and the perfect country house base for exploring the ruggedly beautiful countryside of Connemara. *Directions:* Take the N59 from Galway to Clifden then turn right at the church for the 10-kilometer drive to Rosleague Manor.

ROSLEAGUE MANOR
Owners: Anne Foyle
Letterfrack, Connemara
Co Galway
tel: (095) 41101 fax: (095) 41168
20 ensuite rooms
Double from £80
Open Easter to October
Credit cards: all major
Country house hotel

Kilkenny is a most attractive, historic town, and there is no more perfect a base for exploring its many charms, than from Blanchville House, a 15-minute drive away. Acres of farmland give this handsome Georgian home seclusion. You'll know you've arrived when you see a tall square church tower-like folly. In days gone by it was equipped with clocks and bells and must have been quite a sight to behold. Inside Blanchville House, tall-ceilinged, generously-proportioned rooms are the order of the day, and Monica is particularly proud of having several pieces of furniture that were made for the house. One of these is the glorious half-tester bed that graces the principal bedroom. Apparently Sir James Kearny was fond of waxing and singeing his mustache, an operation he performed in his bed (he was by all accounts a great eccentric who had an aversion to women). One day, while practicing this routine, he set fire to the bedding and narrowly escaped burning the house down. There's a portrait of Sir James in the drawing room which has the lovely wallpaper hung in 1823—here guests enjoy a drink before going in to dine together round the long, polished table. County Kilkenny is particularly lovely and Monica can give you a tourist map which directs you to a great many craftshops. *Directions:* Leave Kilkenny on the N10 (Carlow to Dublin road) and Blanchville House is signposted to your right after 5 kilometers. Pass over the railway crossing, turn left at Connly's Pub, and the house is on your left after 1 kilometer.

BLANCHVILLE HOUSE
Owners: Monica and Tim Phelan
Dunbell
Maddoxtown
Co Kilkenny
tel (056) 27197 fax: (056) 27636
6 rooms, 4 ensuite
From £25 per person B&B
Open March to November
Credit cards: none
Country house

If you are seeking a romantic interlude on a gracious country estate, you can do no better than to choose Longueville House, whose size takes your breath away. Set on a hill overlooking the River Blackwater, this elegant country house offers you the very best of Irish hospitality. It was built by one of Michael O'Callaghan's ancestors, who was spurred on to grander things by a sum of money he received for supporting the British Act of Union. In 1866, a lacy, wrought-iron and glass conservatory was added—filled with baskets of bright summer flowers and palm trees. Today it is a glorious place to dine on a warm summer evening. The adjacent Presidents' Restaurant where portraits of former Irish presidents gaze down benevolently offers the finest of Irish cuisine. The food is mainly from the farm, garden, and river and the kitchen is supervised by son, William. A bottle of wine from the extensive wine list is a delightful accompaniment to your meal—Longueville has Ireland's only vineyard and offers its unique, fruity white wine to guests whenever growing conditions allow. Bedrooms vary in size from enormous to large. All are beautifully decorated and have modern bathrooms. There is a game room including a full-size billiard table. The nearby River Blackwater offers salmon and trout fishing for guests. There are several eighteen-hole golf courses within easy reach of Longueville—Mallow, Killarney, Cork, and Tralee and the links at Ballybunion. *Directions:* The hotel is located on the N72, 5 kilometers west of Mallow on the Killarney road. Shannon airport is 85 kilometers away.

LONGUEVILLE HOUSE
Owners: Jane, Michael, and William O'Callaghan
Mallow
Co Cork
tel: (022) 47156 fax: (022) 47459
16 ensuite rooms
Double from £132
Open mid-March to mid-December
Credit cards: all major
Country house hotel

Standing amidst hundreds of acres of parkland, a half-hour drive from Dublin, Moyglare Manor was built in 1770 as an elegant country mansion. A refined air still pervades the hotel as you step into a world of opulence, where elegant Victorian antiques are flanked by old-fashioned sofas and chairs covered in fabrics that coordinate with the wallpaper and draperies. There's a cluttered, over-furnished look to the drawing room, and whenever I have visited, there has always been a buzz of conversation as groups draw their chairs round the fire or gather in convivial clusters. The dining room occupies three small rooms so there is always an intimate atmosphere. Bedrooms are delightful, all beautifully furnished with many lovely Victorian antiques. The suites are especially large and opulent. Sightseeing attractions within a half-hour drive include Castletown House, Russborough House (with its collection of world famous paintings including the only Vermeer in private hands apart from H. M. The Queen's), and Glendalough, the 6th-century monastic site of St Kevin with its round tower, ruined churches, and high cross. *Directions:* From Dublin take the N4 to Maynooth. Keep right at the Catholic church—the 2-kilometer drive to Moyglare Manor is well signposted.

MOYGLARE MANOR   **NEW**
Owner: Norah Devlin
Manager: Shay Curran
Maynooth
Co Kildare
tel: (01) 6286351 fax: (01) 6285405
17 ensuite rooms
Double from £120
Open all year
Credit cards: all major
Country house hotel

Beth and Ken Sherrard bought Glenview House over 30 years ago as little more than a shell, and worked very hard to restore it, using authentic materials and antiques whenever possible, and created a comfortable family home. Now the children are grown, guests occupy the family's bedrooms. The names of former occupants are on the doors, and family pictures, photo albums, and stuffed toys remain. If you want to languish in a huge tub or drench yourself from a plate-sized shower head, request the room with the Jules-Verne-like, Victorian shower/tub combination—operating instructions essential. If you want wonderful views and lots of space, request Mum and Dad's room with its king-size bed and panoramic view of the wooded valley. Downstairs is a small double room with a bathroom adjoining. In the evening, guests help themselves to drinks from the little honesty bar and enjoy them either on the sheltered patio or in the spacious drawing room with its chairs drawn up cozily by the fire. Beth is happy to provide a three-course dinner. "Must visits" include the whiskey distillery in nearby Midleton and the maritime museum in Cobh. *Directions:* From Midleton take the L35 towards Fermoy for 4 kilometers to a reforested area. Take the first left and immediately right up the hill. Glenview House is the first on the left.

GLENVIEW HOUSE   **NEW**
Owners: Beth and Ken Sherrard
Ballinaclasha
Midleton
Co Cork
tel: (021) 631680 fax: (021) 631680
4 ensuite rooms
From £30 per person B&B
Open all year
Credit cards : MC, VS
Country house

Roundwood House is situated near Mountrath in a scenic spot at the foot of the Slieve Bloom Mountains. The house was built in the 1730s for Anthony Sharp upon his return from America. He attached this elegant Palladian home to his grandfather's simple Quaker cottage which still remains at the back of the house. Roundwood House had pretty much fallen into disrepair by the time it was purchased in the 1970s by the Georgian Society whose careful restoration is being continued by Frank and Rosemarie Kennan who forsook the corporate life of IBM. The gray appearance of the outside of the house belies its colorful interior—bright white and blue for the hall and bold yellows, blues, and reds for the bedrooms—all done in true Georgian style to give a dramatic impact to the lovely, high-ceilinged rooms. Bathrooms and central heating are the only visible 20th-century modifications. Collections of books and paintings and beautiful antique furniture combine with the friendliness of your hosts, Frank and Rosemarie, to make this a most inviting place to stay. There is no need to worry about bringing children along because a portion of the top floor of the house is a nursery with plenty of toys and games to keep children amused for hours. *Directions:* Take the N7 from Dublin to Mountrath and follow signs for the Slieve Bloom Mountains which will bring you to Roundwood House 5 kilometers out of town.

ROUNDWOOD HOUSE
Owners: Frank and Rosemarie Kennan
Mountrath
Co Laois
tel: (0502) 32120 fax: (0502) 32711
6 ensuite rooms
From £35 per person B&B
Open all year
Credit cards: all major
Country house

Moycullen House, of all wooden construction inside, was built in 1900 as a fishing and shooting lodge for Lord Campbell, a Scot who came to western Ireland for his holidays. Philip's mum bought it as a home. Later Philip and Marie did a house exchange with her, and moved here with their six sons. Guests have a large sitting room and dine together 'round the long, oak table—guests are encouraged to bring their own wine and alcoholic beverages. On the night of my visit, dinner was mushroom soup, tarragon chicken with vegetable stirfry, and for dessert, blackcurrant crumble. It is more noticeable that the house is of wooden construction upstairs, where the sloping wooden ceilings give the rooms an attic coziness. Across the hallway from each bedroom is its bathroom (no showers) and you match the plaque on your bedroom door with that of your bathroom—one has a lovely, old-fashioned claw-foot tub. Isolated by 30 acres of rocky garden, rhododendrons, and azaleas, the house has a solitary feel to it. Readers letters back up our experience that the Casburns are only reasonably friendly. Guests can take a day trip to the Aran Islands from Rossaveel or Spiddal. *Directions:* Leave Galway on the N59 (Clifden road) to Moycullen (15 kilometers). Turn left towards Spiddal and Moycullen House is signposted to your left 2 kilometers out of town.

MOYCULLEN HOUSE
Owners: Marie and Philip Casburn
Moycullen
Co Galway
tel: (091) 85566 fax: (091) 85566
5 rooms, 1 ensuite
From £27.50 per person B&B
Open March to October
Credit cards: all major
Country house

Lough Owel Lodge is a modern house set between Lough Owel and a quiet country road that runs into Mullingar. While it is not a house of architectural distinction, this is a quiet country spot where you can cycle down quiet roads, stroll the shores of Lough Owel and generally enjoy the peace and quiet of the center of Ireland. Aideen and Martin Ginnell find that the house works really well for raising a family of four children and providing B&B, for it is divided into two parts, the front being for guests and the back for their family. I particularly appreciated the large carport which sheltered me from the rain as I arrived. A large sitting room with comfortable flowered sofas leads into the dining room with its floor-to-ceiling windows and views of the green garden. Upstairs quite the prettiest bedrooms are the four-poster room with its enormous, almost 2-meter-square bed, and the family suite which consists of a small double bedroom leading to a small twin-bedded room and a large bathroom. Guests are welcome to use the tennis court and enjoy the children's game room. Tullynally Castle, Carrickglass Manor, Belvedere House, Fore Abbey, and Athlone Castle are within an hour's drive. *Directions:* Take the N4 from Dublin towards Sligo. After passing the third exit for Mullingar, Lough Owel Lodge is signposted to your left after 1 kilometer.

LOUGH OWEL LODGE   **NEW**
Owners: Aideen and Martin Ginnell
Cullion
Mullingar
Co Westmeath
tel: (044) 48714 fax: (044) 48714
5 ensuite rooms
From £15 per person B&B
Open March to November
Credit cards: MC, VS
B&B

Mornington House is a most delightful manor house, offering you a glimpse of what it was like to live the life of the landed gentry of Ireland—at a very reasonable price. Warwick O'Hara is the fifth generation of his family to call this home and you are encouraged to make it yours. Family portraits and pictures gaze down upon you as you dine around the enormous dining-room table. Anne has such a reputation for her food that she offers cookery classes locally. Families are welcome and children can be served an early tea. The two front bedrooms are enormous: one has a large brass bed sitting center stage which requires a climb to get into it, while the other has twin brass beds and shares the view across the peaceful grounds. The third bedroom is small only by comparison with the front rooms, and looks out to the side garden and the woods. The oldest wing of the house has two smaller bedrooms which are often offered on a self catering basis in conjunction with a downstairs living room and kitchen. Warwick provides guest with tourist maps that outline quiet country drives through the rolling countryside of central Ireland. *Directions:* From Dublin take the Sligo Road (N4). When you are on the Mullingar bypass, exit for Castlepollard and follow this road for 10 kilometers to Crookedwood where you turn left by the Covert pub. After 2 kilometers turn right and Mornington House is on your right after 1 kilometer.

MORNINGTON HOUSE
Owners: Anne and Warwick O'Hara
Mornington
Multyfarnham
Mullingar
Co Westmeath
tel: (044) 72191 fax: (044) 72338
5 rooms, 4 ensuite
From £25 per person B&B
Open Easter to October
Credit cards: EC, MC, VS
Country house

Dromoland Castle is a spectacular, albeit very expensive, place to spend either your first or last night's stay if you are flying into or out of Shannon airport. Before it became a luxury hotel in 1963, Dromoland Castle saw almost 400 years as the ancestral home of the O'Brien clan. Now it is the luxurious sister hotel of the prestigious Ashford Castle. Jacket and tie for gentlemen are the order of the day after 7:00 pm in the elegant, formal dining room and the book-lined bar where guests often settle after dinner to join in the singing of popular Irish ballads. The sumptuous, ornate drawing room is an ideal haven for morning coffee and afternoon tea. Up the grand staircase are found the hotel's premier rooms and luxurious suites and a portrait gallery of past incumbents of the estate. Smaller cozy rooms are located round a courtyard in the castle oldest part (1736) and have the same amenities as their sumptuous sisters: robes, slippers, masses of toiletries, fruit bowl and a decanter of Irish Mist. Treat yourself to a leisurely breakfast in bed or order dinner from the extensive room service menu (breakfast is not included in the room rates)—the hotel prides itself on its impeccable service. Fishing, horse riding, and bird shooting can be arranged nearby, and tennis courts and Dromoland's golf course are here for you to use. Nearby Bunratty Castle and Folk Park is well worth a visit. *Directions:* The Dromoland Estate is on the N18, Ennis to Limerick road, 13 kilometers north of Shannon airport.

DROMOLAND CASTLE
Manager: Mark Nolan
Dromoland
Newmarket-on-Fergus
Co Clare
tel: (061) 36814 4 fax: (061) 363355
75 ensuite rooms
Double from £232
Open all year
Credit cards: all major
Luxury resort

When Lord Inchquin sold Dromoland Castle in 1963, he moved up the hill to Thomond House, a large Georgian-style mansion that he had built next door. Now it is home to his nephew Conor O'Brien (the present Lord Inchquin and head of the O'Brien chieftancy), his wife, and their two young daughters. And what a lovely home it is, with its high-ceilinged rooms looking out through tall windows to the surrounding countryside. Guests are encouraged to enjoy the comfortable drawing room, breakfast in the dining room, and watch television amidst the children's toys in the study. The sweeping staircase leads to the upper gallery and the bedrooms which are all elegantly kitted out and offer views of the parkland or the adjacent castle. There are a great many places to eat nearby: you can walk down the driveway to Dromoland Castle and enjoy a superb formal meal in their elegant dining room or drive a few kilometers to Durty Nelly's and enjoy casual fare in this traditional Irish pub with its sawdust-strewn floors. You are welcome to roam over the 1,000-acre estate, wandering along the banks of the River Rine and through the green parkland and woodland. Farther afield lie the dramatic Cliffs of Moher and the Burren with its rocky landscapes. *Directions:* The Dromoland Estate is on the N18, Ennis to Limerick road, 13 kilometers north of Shannon airport. The entrance to Thomond House is south of Dromoland Castle.

THOMOND HOUSE   **NEW**
Owners: Helen and Conor Inchquin
Dromoland
Newmarket-on-Fergus
Co Clare
tel: (061) 368304 fax: (061) 368285
5 ensuite rooms
From £75 per person B&B
Open all year
Credit cards: all major
Country house

Isolated by a tall hedge of cypress trees, Creacon Lodge and its pretty garden look for all the world like a little bit of England transported to Ireland. The inside is just as charming as out, with everything in decorator-perfect order. Guests can relax, enjoy a drink, watch TV, or listen to music in the sitting room with its comfy sofas and chairs arranged around the fire. With advance notice, Josephine is happy to provide an evening meal, and for those sailing on the morning ferry, an early breakfast is always available (Creacon Lodge is only a 40-kilometer drive from Rosslare Harbor). Up a narrow flight of stairs, the little bedrooms with their sloping ceilings are tucked under the roof of the house and their tiny, floor-level windows offer glimpses of the garden. Across the courtyard three bedrooms, in the cottage, offer more spacious accommodation and immaculate shower rooms. A further building, the Gatehouse, contains two bedrooms which I did not enjoy because they had skylights instead of windows. Ten minutes away is John F. Kennedy Park. The nearby Hook peninsula with its secluded coves has the oldest lighthouse in Europe. *Directions:* From Wexford take the N25 New Ross to Cork road. Just before reaching New Ross turn left on the R733 signposted John F. Kennedy Park (do not take the first left for JFK Park). After 5 kilometers turn left for Creacon Lodge.

CREACON LODGE   **NEW**
Owner: Josephine Flood
Creacon Lower
New Ross
Co Wexford
tel: (051) 21897 fax: (051) 22560
8 ensuite rooms
From £20 per person B&B
Open all year
Credit cards: MC, VS
B&B

A cottage, a church, and Hanora's Cottage Guesthouse nestle beside the tumbling Nire River in this delightfully wild and isolated spot on the edge of the Comeragh Mountains. The house is of modern, rather boxy, construction with a tidy sitting room and a restaurant downstairs, and upstairs, an array of small color-coordinated bedrooms with soft-pastel walls and matching drapes, bedcovers, and towels. Each bedroom has TV, hairdryer, tea and coffee makings, and a small shower room. The nicest accommodation is offered by the more spacious Room 8 whose bathroom contains a jacuzzi tub. Son, Eoin (pronounced Owen) offers a set, four-course dinner with lots of choices for starters and main courses. Packed lunches, maps, and directions are available for walks that range from leisurely woodland rambles to challenging hill walks. Try to plan your stay to include a Saturday so you can accompany Seamus and CJ, the family dog, on their ramble and hear stories of the folklore and history of the rocky, heather-clad Comeraghs. If you're not worn out by walking, visit the local pubs that offer music and dancing. *Directions:* From Clonmel or Dungarvan, follow the R672 as far as Ballymacarbry village where you turn left into the Nire valley at Melody's Lounge Bar. Travel 5.6 kilometers: Hanora's is beside the church just before the stone bridge.

HANORA'S COTTAGE GUESTHOUSE **NEW**
Owners: Mary and Seamus Wall
Nire Valley
Via Clonmel
Co Waterford
tel: (052) 36134 fax: (052) 36540
8 ensuite rooms
From £22 per person B&B
Open all year
Credit cards: EC, MC, VS
Guesthouse

Three things combine to make Cnoc na Curra an exceptional bed and breakfast—a stunning location on the shore of Lough Corrib, a delightfully decorated house, and the warm welcome that Gene Larkin gives to her guests. After showing you to your room, Gene invites you to join her for tea either in the attractive sitting room or on the long, covered verandah that overlooks the island-dotted lough. Breakfast is the only meal served, but Gene has menus on hand from several of the many restaurants in town. Two of the very attractive bedrooms are on the ground floor: in one, the bedroom leads directly into the bathroom and through French windows onto a private patio. The upstairs bedroom has a large picture window overlooking the lake. Gene does not want guests to hide away in their bedroom so she tempts them to use the lovely sitting room, all decked out in shades of green, by having lots of books and information on the area on hand here. Salmon, trout, and coarse fishing are a big draw at Lough Corrib, and Gene and Declan have a small boat with engine that people can hire by the day—or they will arrange for ghillies to take you fishing. Non-fisher types can enjoy spectacular drives through the rugged Galway countryside and sightseeing trips to islands on the lough. *Directions:* Oughterard is 26 kilometers from Galway on the N59. As you enter the town turn right opposite the Esso station, and Cnoc na Curra is the first house on your left after 1 kilometer.

CNOC NA CURRA
Owners: Gene and Declan Larkin
Pier Road
Oughterard
Co Galway
tel: (091) 82225
3 ensuite rooms
From £17.50 per person
Open mid-May to mid-September
Credit cards: none
B&B

Guests at Currarevagh House find themselves entering a world reminiscent of the turn of the century. Tranquillity reigns supreme and the good old-fashioned way is the way things are done at Currarevagh House. However, do not be afraid that you will be deprived of central heating and private bathrooms, for this is not the case. Bedrooms are all priced the same. If you book well in advance you may be able to secure room 1 or 3 in the old house or room 16 in the new wing with their lake views. Try to arrive by 4:30 pm when tea and cakes are served. You will then have enough time for a brisk walk to make room for dinner at 8 pm. A gong announces dinner is served, and while there are no choices, the helpings are of generous proportions. A tempting breakfast buffet of meats, cheeses, and traditional cooked breakfast dishes is spread on the sideboard, and the hotel is happy to pack you a picnic lunch. As a special treat for those who are returning that night, they will pack it in a quaint old tin box bound by a leather strap. It's all very old-fashioned and un-decorator-perfect, but I must admit that I thoroughly enjoyed it—the Hodgsons really do manage to create the illusion of being back in Victorian times. Harry can arrange for fishing on the adjacent Lough Corrib, the second largest lake in Ireland, which is a haven for fishermen. *Directions:* From Galway take the N59 to Oughterard, turn right in the center of the village, and follow the lakeshore for the 6-kilometer drive to the house.

CURRAREVAGH HOUSE
Owners: June and Harry Hodgson
Oughterard, Connemara
Co Galway
tel: (091) 82312 fax: (091) 82731
15 ensuite rooms
Double from £93
Open April to October
Credit cards: none
Country house hotel

Ardeen was an especially welcome haven after we explored the Donegal coast on a particularly gloomy, wet summer's day. This attractive Victorian house was once the town doctor's home. Anne Campbell and her husband had always admired Ardeen's airy rooms and large riverside garden, so when it came up for sale, they jumped at the opportunity to call it home. Breakfast around the large dining-room table is the only meal that Anne prepares, though she is happy to offer advice on where to eat in Ramelton. Guests can plan their sightseeing from the warmth of the sitting room. Upstairs a sunny yellow double room faces the water and has a lovely ensuite shower room. A twin room enjoys a small shower room and the pretty peach double and an additional twin room share a large rather dated bathroom. The adjacent stable has been converted to a snug holiday cottage with an exposed stone living room, attractive kitchen, and two attic bedrooms. Ardeen is an ideal base for exploring the Donegal coastline and visiting Glenveagh National Park and the Glebe Art Gallery with its fine collection of Irish paintings. *Directions:* If you are arriving from Donegal, take the N56 to Letterkenny and on the outskirts of the town look for the T72, signposted for Rathmullen. It's an 11-kilometer drive to Ramelton. When you reach the river turn right, following the bank, and Ardeen is on your right.

ARDEEN
Owner: Anne Campbell
Ramelton
Co Donegal
tel: (074) 51243
4 rooms, 2 ensuite
From £17.50 per person B&B
Open Easter to September
Credit cards: AX
B&B

When they built an elegant, modern home on their farm over ten years ago, Anne and Gerald Thompson called it Magherasollus, translated from the Irish as "the plain of light," for the house was specially designed so that it captures the brightest of light all day long. Anne had always lived in old homes and has a lot of lovely family antiques so it was important to her that, while the exterior of her home was modern, the interior should be traditional. The sitting room with its pale green sofas and chairs drawn 'round the fire opens up to the dining room with its lovingly polished table and dresser, and both enjoy spectacular views across rolling, green countryside to distant hills. Up the staircase, the master bedroom has a sparkling bathroom and enjoys a small balcony. Two additional bedrooms share a large bathroom. From this lush countryside spot you can easily venture to the rugged Donegal coastline where little cottages snuggle in every sheltered spot and the views (on clear days) are spectacular. To the northeast, fast roads lead you to the Antrim coast and the Giant's Causeway. *Directions:* From Donegal take the N15 towards Letterkenny through Ballybofey. After 5 kilometers take R236 through Convoy to Raphoe. From Raphoe take the Derry road and after 2 kilometers Magherasollus Farmhouse is on your left.

MAGHERASOLLUS FARMHOUSE
Owners: Anne and Gerald Thompson
Raphoe
Co Donegal
tel: (074) 45265
3 rooms, 1 ensuite
From £14.50 per person B&B
Open June, July, and August
Credit cards: none
Farmhouse B&B

Rathmullan House has a perfect setting amidst acres of lovingly tended gardens that slope down to a sandy beach, with views of the mountains across Lough Swilly. This large, rambling country house is decorated in a variety of styles from Egyptian (in the new wing), through traditional country house, to Bedouin in the dining pavilion where vast meters of fabric have been gathered across the ceiling to give a tentlike appearance to the three interconnecting rooms. A three- or four-course dinner is offered with enough selections in each course to satisfy the most discerning diner. After dinner coffee is offered on a help-yourself basis in the coffee lounge. Most spacious, attractive accommodation is offered in the large rooms above the Egyptian baths (saltwater swimming pool, sauna and steam room). Bedrooms in the main house are a mixed bunch varying from snug attic under the eaves to large bedrooms with bay windows that have views to the lough. Downstairs is a convivial cellar bar. A 10% service charge is added to your bill. Adjacent to the hotel is a complex of holiday cottages. Rathmullan is a particularly attractive village and there are some spectacular drives round the Fanad peninsula. Inland lies Glenveagh National Park, and the Glebe Art Gallery. *Directions:* From Donegal take the N15 to Ballybofey, then the N56 to the outskirts of Letterkenny, through Ramelton, and follow the shores of Lough Swilly through Rathmullan. The house is on your right as you leave the village.

RATHMULLAN HOUSE
Owners: Robin and Bob Wheeler
Rathmullan
Letterkenny
Co Donegal
tel: (074) 58188 fax: (074) 58200
23 rooms, 21 ensuite
Double from £88
Open mid-March to November
Credit cards: all major
Country house hotel

"There is nothing which has yet been contrived by man by which so much happiness is produced as by a good inn"—Hunter's Hotel has adopted Samuel Johnson's words as a creed and they certainly describe it. Dating back to the 1720s, the hotel retains its old-world charm with creaking wooden floorboards, polished tile floors, old prints, beams, ancient sofas covered in old-fashioned chintz, and antique furniture. The Gelletlie family have owned the inn since 1820, and now Tom and Richard Gelletlie (the fifth generation) enthusiastically assist their mother, Maureen. There is a delightful feeling of another age which endures in the tradition of vast, Sunday roast lunches (1 pm prompt: book ahead) and afternoon teas of oven-fresh scones and strawberry jam—a particularly delightful feast when enjoyed in the garden on a warm summer's afternoon. Most of the attractively decorated bedrooms overlook the flower-filled gardens stretching beside the hotel down to the River Vartry. Room 17, a ground-floor room with a private garden entrance, stands out as a particular favorite. Some of the country's most interesting gardens and houses are a short drive away: Powerscourt with its grand gardens, Mount Usher with its informal gardens, Russborough with its famous art collection, and Avondale House, the home of Charles Stewart Parnell. *Directions:* Take the N11 from Dublin to Rathnew and turn left in the village for the 1-kilometer drive to Hunter's Hotel.

HUNTER'S HOTEL **NEW**
Owners: The Gelletlie family
Rathnew
Co Wicklow
tel: (0404) 40106 fax: (0404) 40338
16 ensuite rooms
From £42.50 per person B&B
Open all year
Credit cards: all major
Inn

Tinakilly House maintains the purpose for which it was designed—gracious living. The house was built in the 1870s by Captain Robert Halpin, the commander of the ship *Great Eastern* which laid the first telegraph cable connecting Europe to America. Tinakilly House's ornate staircase is reputed to be a copy of the one on this ship. Whether or not this is true is a matter of conjecture, but the captain certainly spared no expense when he built this classical house with its fine, pitch-pine doors and shutters and ornate plasterwork ceilings. William and Bee Powers bought the house as a family home, but found the cost of restoration and its size too large, so decided to open it as a luxurious country house hotel. They have done a splendid job, extending the home and adding rooms that fit in perfectly, furnishing the house with appropriate Victorian furniture, and adding a welcoming charm to the place. Five of the bedrooms have four-poster beds, while half the suites including the admiral's suite have breathtaking sea views. Rooms tucked into the original attics, are snug and country-cozy and proportionately less expensive. There are some lovely walks on the grounds and Tinakilly is an ideal countryside base for exploring Dublin, Glendalough, and the Wicklow Mountains. *Directions:* From Dublin take the N11 (Wexford road) to Rathnew village. Turn left, towards Wicklow, and the entrance to the hotel is on your left as you leave the village.

TINAKILLY HOUSE
Owners: Bee and William Powers
Rathnew
Co Wicklow
tel: (0404) 69274 fax: (0404) 67806
29 ensuite rooms
Double from £116
Open all year
Credit cards: all major
Country house hotel

Coopershill was built in 1774, and has always been home to the O'Hara family. Continuing a tradition begun by Joan O'Hara, Brian and Lindy welcome guests to their lovely home through the massive front door, into the stove-warmed hall whose flagged floor is topped by an Oriental rug, and where rain gear hangs at the ready. Beyond lies a parade of lovely rooms tastefully decorated and beautifully furnished with grand, antique furniture, much of which is as old as the house itself. All but two of the bedrooms have the original four-poster or half-tester beds, but of course, with modern mattresses. All the bedrooms are large and have private bathrooms, though one is across the hall. Ancestors' portraits gaze down upon you in the dining room, set with tables to accommodate individual parties. The dinner is excellent and the main course might be local lamb or wild salmon with hollandaise sauce. Afterwards, guests chat 'round the fire over coffee. Coopershill offers the best of both worlds—the luxury of a country house hotel and the warmth of a home. Secluded by 500 acres of farm and woodland, there are many delightful walks, and since no shooting is allowed, wildlife is abundant. Boating and trout and coarse fishing are available on the River Arrow which flows through the property. Beyond the estate, there is enough sightseeing to justify spending a week. *Directions:* From Dublin take the N4 to Drumfin (18 kilometers south of Sligo). Turn right towards Riverstown and Coopershill is on your left 1 kilometer before the village.

COOPERSHILL
Owners: Lindy and Brian O'Hara
Riverstown
Co Sligo
tel: (071) 65108 fax: (071) 65466
7 rooms, 6 ensuite
From £42.50 per person B&B
Open mid-March to October
Credit cards: EC, MC, VS
Country house

Margaret and Dick Johnson have been used to a house full of children, for between them they have nine. Dick is the local vet and now that their family is grown, Margaret has redecorated bedrooms, added shower rooms, and opened their delightful old home to guests. Creaking polished pine floors are topped with rugs, rooms are furnished with antiques, and guests are welcomed as friends. Guests have a comfortable sitting room where they can chat round the fire and relax after dinner round the large oval table. Dinner might be a mackerel soufflé, beef bourguignon with salad and new potatoes, and for dessert, cheese or profiteroles with raspberry sauce. All but the small single bedroom (bathroom down the hall) have snug ensuite shower rooms. The front bedrooms, a twin and a double, offer the most spacious quarters with lots of room for suitcases and a writing table and chair. Ballyteigue House is about an hour-and-a-half drive from Shannon Airport. Margaret finds that guests often use this countryside base for taking day trips to Cashel and Killarney, 1½ hours away. Closer at hand, lie Adare (the prettiest village in Ireland) and Bunratty with its interesting folk park. *Directions:* Charlieville is on the N20 between Limerick and Mallow. Travel 8 kilometers north of the town and turn left at the signpost for Ballyteigue House. Pass Rockhill church and Ballyteigue House is on your right after 500 meters.

BALLYTEIGUE HOUSE   **NEW**
Owners: Margaret and Dick Johnson
Rockhill
Bruree
Co Limerick
tel: (063) 90575
5 rooms, 4 ensuite
From £18 per person B&B
Closed Christmas
Credit cards: EC, MC, VS
Farmhouse B&B

Smugglers Creek Inn is a lively pub sitting high above Rossnowlagh beach, the vast sandy expanse that is reputedly the best surfing beach in Ireland. It's an energetic place where there's always the background music of soft rock or jazz—on Friday evenings there's often a live jazz session which starts at 10 pm and finishes at midnight. Pine benches, chairs, and tables, and a cozy fire flanked by a blackened kettle combine with nautical memorabilia to create an inviting ambiance. An identical menu is available in the bar, conservatory, or quaint little dining room (no smoking) whose tables are topped with starched linen tablecloths. Lots of emphasis is given to seafood, but there are steaks and even sausage and chips for children. Upstairs the bedrooms are cottagey in size, furnished with old pine, and each accompanied by either a spotlessly modern shower or bathroom. I particularly enjoyed the three front bedrooms with their wide ocean views. Good roads quickly speed you into Donegal town where Magees is famous for its tweeds, and parking is hard to come by. A picturesque day trip takes you into Northern Ireland to the Marble Arch Caves and Florence Court, an 18th-century mansion famous for its decorative ceilings. *Directions:* Rossnowlagh is on the coast between Donegal and Ballyshannon. Smugglers Creek Inn is about 8 kilometers north of Ballyshannon on the coast road, signposted from the country road that runs out of sight of the beach.

SMUGGLERS CREEK INN **NEW**
Owner: Conor Britton
Rossnowlagh
Co Donegal
tel: (072) 52366
5 ensuite rooms
From £19.50 per person B&B
Open all year
Credit cards: EC, MC, VS
Inn

In summer, the driveway of Rosturk Woods is lined with wild, red fuchsias which lead you to the low, white house hugging a vast expanse of firm, sandy beach on the shores of Clew Bay. Home to Louisa and Alan Stoney and their young family, the house has the feel of an old cottage, though it is only a few years old. Bedrooms have stripped pine doors and several have pine-paneled, sloping ceilings. There's a lot of old-pine furniture, antique pieces, attractive prints and fabrics. The house cleverly divides so that a wing of two bedrooms, a living room, and a kitchen can be closed off and used as self-catering accommodation. Alan works at the local fishery and grew up in the imposing castle next door, while Louisa's parents live up the road. Dinner is available with advance notice, though Louisa finds that guests often prefer to walk to a small restaurant down the road. Louisa can sometimes direct you to nearby places where traditional Irish music is played. You can hire a boat for a full- or half-day trip on Clew Bay. In contrast to the lush green fields and long sandy beaches that hug Clew Bay, a short drive brings you to the wilder, more rugged scenery of Achill Island. To the south lie the interesting towns of Newport and Westport. *Directions:* From Westport take the N59 through Newport towards Achill Island. Before you arrive in Mulrany, cross the Owengarve River and after 500 meters turn left into the woodland to Rosturk Woods.

ROSTURK WOODS **NEW**
Owners: Louisa and Alan Stoney
Rosturk
Mulrany
Co Mayo
tel: (098) 36264 fax: (098) 36264
5 rooms, 4 ensuite
From £18 per person B&B
Open April to November
Credit cards: EC, MC, VS
B&B

Eileen and Johann Thieme have filled their home with antiques, collectibles, and mementos from their many years of living in Saudi Arabia and Zambia. Oriental rugs of every shape and size grace walls, floors, and chairs—Room 2 has rugs as bedspreads while Room 1 has a large carpet as a headboard above its 6-foot-wide bed. Clocks aplenty are to be found in the living room and Room 3 has at least a dozen on its shelves. Shepherds Wood is cottagey in its design, with polished floors, raftered ceilings, and doors made from lapping thin strips of wood with the bark still showing. Relax in the large sitting room and enjoy meals in the adjoining conservatory with its high-back wicker chairs (evening meals for a minimum of four guests). Breakfast is an adventure with a choice of either traditional Irish fare or a vast array of alternatives, amongst them German breakfast pancakes, Indonesian bananas, and Eggs Benedict. In July and August you can enjoy the outdoor swimming pool. A delightful, self-catering chalet sits beside the swimming pool in the orchard. There are lovely walks through the acres of wooded grounds. Birr Castle with its famous gardens is a short drive away. *Directions:* Take the N52 from Tullamore and travel 6 kilometers towards Birr, turning left at the brown signpost for Shepherds Wood at Screggan. The gate to Shepherds Wood is on your right (in the woodland) after 1 kilometer.

SHEPHERDS WOOD   **NEW**
Owners: Eileen and Johann Thieme
Screggan
Tullamore
Co Offaly
tel: (0506) 21499
4 ensuite rooms
From £18 per person B&B
Open March to October
Credit cards: MC, VS
B&B

Ballymaloe House is a rambling, 17th-century manor house built onto an old Norman keep surrounded by lawns, a small golf course kept cropped by grazing sheep, and 400 acres of farmland. This has been the Allens' family home since 1948 and over the last 25 years Myrtle Allen has set the standards of food and service in Irish country houses. They have an international reputation for their food and hospitality—yet everything is decidedly simple and homey. Guests gather before dinner in the lounge to make their selections from the set menu which offers four or five choices for each of the courses. The bedrooms in the main house come in all shapes and sizes, from large and airy to cozy and paneled. Surrounding a courtyard, the smaller, stable bedrooms offer country-cottage charm, sprigged flowered wallpaper, and beamed ceilings for those on the upper floor. Most unusual accommodations are in the doll-sized gatekeeper's cottage which is just large enough to have a bathroom on the ground floor and a ladder to the twin-bedded room above, with its tiny, log-burning fireplace. Darina Allen came here to learn cooking and stayed to marry son, Tim and found the Ballymaloe Cookery School in the courtyard of her nearby home. Her courses, the television programs, *Simply Delicious,* and cook books have done much to spread the Ballymaloe style of cooking. *Directions:* Ballymaloe is signposted from the N25 (Cork to Waterford road). Ballymaloe is 3 kilometers beyond Cloyne on the Ballycotton Road (R629).

BALLYMALOE HOUSE
Owners: Myrtle and Ivan Allen
Shanagarry
Midleton
Co Cork
tel: (021) 652531 fax: (021) 652021
30 ensuite rooms
Double from £110
Closed for Christmas
Credit cards: all major
Country house hotel

Friends were aghast when Suzanne and Dominic Lee told them that they were buying an Irish farmhouse that had not been occupied for 25 years, and that they were going to offer bed and breakfast in the tumbled-down barn. Two years and a lot of hard work have seen their vision realized and what was derelict is now delightful, full of simple rustic charm. The sturdy, stone barn is home to three very simple, rustic rooms, each with its own entrance. Dominic made the beds, chests of drawers, and little closets, highlighting their simple country charm with either blue or green to coordinate with the duvets and window blinds. At meal times guests congregate in the cottage 'round an old farmhouse table in front of a log stove to enjoy vegetarian food. To tempt guests to stay with them for longer, Suzanne and Dominic have organized cycling holidays in combination with a stay at Gabriel Cottage. They provide user-friendly trail bikes, maps, waterproofs, and in the unlikely event of a breakdown or exhaustion, "rescue service." They have cycled all the loops you explore and, once you are beyond the main Cork to Skibbereen road, awaiting your exploration are peaceful lanes and brightly painted villages such as Baltimore, once looted by pirates, or Castletownshend, where Edith Somerville and Violet Martin wrote *The Experiences of an Irish RM* under the pseudonym Martin Ross. *Directions:* Gabriel Cottage is on the N71, on the left, 3 kilometer from Skibbereen on the Cork road.

GABRIEL COTTAGE
Owners: Suzanne and Dominic Lee
Smorane
Skibbereen
Co Cork
tel: (028) 22521
3 ensuite rooms
From £17.50 per person B&B
Open May to September
Credit cards: none
Farmhouse B&B

Kee's Hotel is an old commercial and posting house was bought by Willie Kee in the latter part of the 19th century, beginning a tradition of hospitality which continues today into the fourth generation of the Kee family. Over the years there have been many changes, but none more dramatic than in the last few years when a luxurious swimming pool, health club, and larger, executive rooms have been added to the rear of the hotel as well a large car park, essential in this small, busy town. To complete the new look, all the remaining bedrooms have received a complete facelift with light, fitted furniture, pastel-painted walls, and matching, blue-flowered drapes and bedspreads. Each room is accompanied by a modern bathroom. All the guestrooms are very attractive, though I think it is worth the few extra pounds to plump for one of the more spacious, tailored, executive rooms. Soak up a traditional Irish atmosphere and enjoy the bustle and excellent food of the Rafters or Tapestry restaurants, or the Scenes Bar with its flagstone floor and open log fire. Guests are welcome to use the large indoor swimming pool and health club. Stranolar is perfect for venturing out on day trips around Donegal. If you are traveling to or from the Antrim coast (Giant's Causeway), it's an ideal place to break your journey. *Directions:* From Donegal take the N15 towards Letterkenny to the twin towns of Ballybofey and Stranolar where Kee's Hotel is on your right. There is a large car park to the rear of the hotel.

KEE'S HOTEL
Owners: The Kee family
Stranolar
Ballybofey
Co Donegal
tel: (074) 31018 fax: (074) 31917
35 ensuite rooms
Double from £60
Open all year
Credit cards: all major
Family hotel

Anthony and Katie Hamilton had always admired their friend's home, Killyreagh, so when he offered to sell it to them they took the plunge, and after carrying out extensive refurbishing and modernization, moved here with their two young children. Guests enjoy a luxurious drawing room all decked out in soft pastels. By contrast, the hunters-green dining room hung with lovely bird prints is very masculine and it is here that guests enjoy dinner and breakfast. Bedrooms and their prices range from a modest twin room to a grand master bedroom with its antique four-poster bed, watched over by ancestral portraits (a small, single bedroom off the bathroom is perfect for a child). Guests are welcome to use the modern, all-weather tennis court. The lodge by the entry gate which contains two bedrooms, a sitting room, and a kitchen is rented on a weekly, self-catering basis. There are some peaceful drives around nearby Lough Erne and three very interesting National Trust properties: Castle Coole, a restored Palladian mansion, Florence Court, a riot of rococo plasterwork, and the romantic ruins of Old Crom Castle. The Marble Arch Caves with their stalagmites and stalactites are a nearby attraction. *Directions:* Tamlaght is just off the A4, 5 kilometers east of Enniskillen. Turn over the bridge and follow the road through the council estate into the countryside. Pass a farm and turn left at the gatehouse into Killyreagh's driveway.

KILLYREAGH
Owners: Lord Anthony and Lady Hamilton
Tamlaght
Enniskillen
Co Fermanagh
tel: (01365)87721 fax: (01365) 87122
5 rooms, 1 ensuite
From £30 to £50 per person B&B
Open all year
Credit cards: none
Country house

Set in eleven acres of garden with vast lawns sweeping down to a lake, Tempo Manor is a spectacular spot. Built in 1867 by John Langham's great-great-grandfather, Sir William Emerson-Tennent, the house is as attractive inside, as it is out. Ancient armaments and hunting trophies line the paneled walls of the entrance halls, while overhead hangs great-granddad's wooden propeller from his World War I airplane. Much of the furniture was made for the house—a redoubtable collection of ancestors portraits occupies a great deal of wall space. Portraits of the current generation are confined to holiday snaps in the downstairs loo. John and Sarah are young, enthusiastic and putting a great deal of work into the restoration of their lovely home. While two of the bedrooms had grand four poster beds, by the time you arrive, John may have them installed in all the bedrooms (he was busy restoring them when I visited in May 94). A house party atmosphere is the order of the day and John joins his guests for drinks before dinner, accompanied as he always is by his Alsatian, Keyneton. Edward, Sarah's family butler has retired to live with them and may be on hand to serve dinner. The gardens and acres of woodlands provide the opportunity for peaceful walks. Within an hours drive are three National Trust houses: Florence Court, Coole Castle and Crom Castle. *Directions:* From Belfast take the M1 motorway west. At Fivemiletown turn right for Tempo and left in the town signpost Brookeboro. Tempo Manor is at the first gatehouse on the left signposted: "No Admittance."

TEMPO MANOR   **NEW**
Owners: Sarah and John Langham
Tempo
Co Fermanagh
tel: (013655) 41450 fax: (013655) 41202
4 bedrooms with private bathrooms
From £45 per person B&B
Closed Christmas
Credit cards: EC, MC, VS
Country house

Riverrun House looks for all the world like an old farmhouse, when in fact it was built just a few years ago using a traditional farmhouse design with old windows, doors, and roof slates. The delightful deception continues inside where old-fashioned doors, deep skirting boards, and a traditional fireplace add appeal to the little sitting room. Bedrooms are charming—plainly and unfussily decorated and all have sparkling modern bathrooms with showers. Two downstairs rooms have farmhouse half-doors and private patios. End rooms are larger. Breakfast is the only meal served and guests usually walk the few yards to Paddy Pub and The Derg. Riverrun House has a tennis court and bikes for guests to borrow—there's no shortage of quiet country lanes. You can hire a boat for the day and enjoy Lough Derg. Further afield lies Bunratty Castle and Folk Park, and Clonmacnois the 6th century monastic settlement on the Shannon River. *Directions:* Nenagh is on the N7, Limerick to Dublin road. Leave the main road in Nenagh and travel through Borrisokane and Ballinderry to Terryglass. Riverrun House is opposite the bridge in the village.

RIVERRUN HOUSE
Owners: Lucy and Tom Sanders
Terryglass
Nenagh
Co Tipperary
tel: (067) 22125 fax: (067) 22187
6 ensuite rooms
From £22.50 per person B&B
Closed Christmas
Credit cards: all major
B&B

Jerpoint House and its surrounding farm buildings, built around 1780, had fallen into a state of disrepair when they were bought by a British artist and his Dutch wife who converted the complex into avant-garde homes. Oonagh and Harry O'Neill realized that Jerpoint House could not be reconverted to a traditional Georgian home, so they revamped some of its more eccentric aspects. Visitors usually find Oonagh in her sunny kitchen, formerly the grand entry hall, baking the bread that she sells to local shops. Guests have their own entry and are given a door key so that they can come and go as they please. Relax by the fire, watch TV, or spread your maps out on the dining table in the high-ceilinged sitting room with its watermelon-colored walls and tall, red-shuttered windows. Up the wrought iron staircase (Oonagh feels this makes the house unsuitable for children under 12) are three small bedrooms each identically decorated with patterned bedspreads and drapes, and accompanied by a modern shower room. Breakfast is the only meal served and guests often dine in Hunters Yard at Mount Juliet hotel or at Pat Kavanagh's pub in Thomastown. The ruins of Jerpoint Abbey are nearby. A few kilometers distant lie Kilkenny and Waterford. *Directions:* From Kilkenny take the N10 (Waterford road) for 13 kilometers through Stoneyford. Beyond the village turn left, signposted Mount Juliet, and Jerpoint is on your left 500 meters beyond the hotel entrance.

JERPOINT HOUSE   **NEW**
Owners: Oonagh and Harry O'Neill
Thomastown
Co Kilkenny
tel: (056) 24649
3 ensuite rooms
From £15 per person B&B
Open all year
Credit cards: none
B&B

As you enter Mount Juliet estate, you may catch glimpses of pheasants feeding along the driveway or see riders enjoying a pony trek through the 1,500 acre walled estate. A narrow, mellow-stone bridge takes you across the River Nore to the heart of Ireland's premier luxury resort. Guests need not travel beyond the estate's boundaries, for here you can enjoy swimming, relaxing at the Spa and Leisure Centre, tennis, croquet, archery, clay pigeon shooting, fishing for salmon and trout along the River Nore, riding along kilometers of idyllic park and woodland trails, while golfers can sharpen up their game at the David Leadbetter Golf Academy before taking on the magnificent Jack Nicklaus designed championship golf course. With lawns tumbling down to the river and overlooking fenced pastures and vast woodlands, Mount Juliet was built as a grand home for the Earls of Carrick in the 1760s. Its numerous rooms have received a complete and elegant revamping to provide quiet lounges, distinguished dining, clubby bars, a parade of deluxe bedrooms, and two superlative suites. More casual accommodation and dining is available in Hunters Yard, a stableyard-like complex beside the golf clubhouse. *Directions:* Thomastown is on the N9, Kilkenny to Waterford road. The 5-kilometer drive to the hotel is signposted from the center of town.

MOUNT JULIET
Manager: James O'Hara
Thomastown
Co Kilkenny
tel: (056) 24455 fax: (056) 24523
32 ensuite rooms
Double from £195, Suite from £295
Open all year
Credit cards: all major
Luxury resort

This 200 acre dairy and cattle farm is a delight for adults and children alike: as well as farm activities there are pony rides (on a leading rein), tennis courts, and a children's game room. Such is the popularity of the place that people who came as children, are now returning with their children. Whenever David Kent is not occupied with farm matters, he loves to talk to visitors and discuss the farm and what to do and see in the area. (The Waterford crystal factory is a big draw and Margaret is happy to make an appointment to tour.) Margaret is one of those people who shows her appreciation of her guests by feeding them lavishly. She delights in the preparation of dishes of beef from the farm and homegrown fruits (strawberries, raspberries, gooseberries, apples, and rhubarb, to name but a few) and vegetables—her specialty is her homemade ice cream. Her bountiful breakfasts have won her national awards. Guests are served after-dinner coffee in the lounge and often linger for discussions around the fireside. Upstairs, the bedrooms are delightfully decorated. Two small twin rooms are perfect for children and share a shower room. The four ensuite rooms have spanking new bathrooms and three have extra beds making them ideal for family accommodation. *Directions:* To find the house, take the road from Waterford toward Dunmore East. After about 6 kilometers, at the Maxol garage, take the left fork toward Passage East. Foxmount Farm is signposted on the right 500 meters from the Maxol garage.

FOXMOUNT FARM
Owners: Margaret and David Kent
Dunmore East Road
Waterford
Co Waterford
tel: (051) 74308
6 rooms, 4 ensuite
From £18.50 per person B&B
Open April to mid-October
Credit cards: none
Farmhouse B&B

Arriving at Waterford Castle by means of an adorable little ferry (which takes you and your car over the waters of the River Suir to your private island retreat), makes a stay here especially appealing. Edward Fitzgerald who translated *The Rubiayat of Omar Khayyam*, lived here in what was for many generations, his family home. The castellated parapets and ancient gargoyles of this warm, creeper-covered mansion have never known a shot fired in battle. Erected during the time when the fashion for mock-Gothic architecture was at its peak, it was built as a luxurious family home. The interior is just as striking: the crest above the cavernous stone fireplace in the Great Hall is reproduced in vivid color in the carpet. A quiet aura of dignified opulence pervades the hotel where you are assisted by young, well-trained, attentive staff. There are sumptuous suites to spread out in—the Presidential is particularly decadent. The Ormonde Room, a spacious, high-ceilinged twin decorated in shades of peach with tall windows overlooking the golf course was my favorite superior room—others by comparison lacked character. There are no standard rooms. A portion of the 300-acre island is a par-72 golf course. You can indulge in forest walk, fishing, tennis, and swimming (a simple clubhouse houses an indoor pool). *Directions:* From Waterford take the road towards Dunmore East for 3 kilometers to a left-hand turn signposted Waterford Castle. The road ends at the ferry.

WATERFORD CASTLE
Owner: Eddie Kearns
Ballinakill
Waterford
Co Waterford
tel: (051) 78203 fax: (051) 79316
19 ensuite rooms
Double from £280
Open all year
Credit cards: all major
Luxury resort

Westport is one of the few architecturally pre-designed towns in Ireland. Its architect, James Wyatt, made the most of the site: the river is walled in and tree-lined, and he designed an attractive, octagonal town center. The waterfront lies away from the town, many of its old buildings transformed into pubs and restaurants. Just a short drive beyond the waterfront lies Wilmaur, a purposely built bed and breakfast with Clew Bay dotted with little green islands at its front and Croagh Patrick (the cone-shaped holy mountain of Ireland) at its rear. A plant-filled entryway gives way to a large two-story hallway with a its soft Oriental carpet in pinks and greens matching perfectly the green carpets that lead to the bedrooms and upstairs to the large sitting room where sofas and chairs are invitingly drawn around the fire. Guestrooms and the breakfast room are all on the ground floor. Bedrooms are all similar in size and have a small shower room (two have a double and one twin bed, and three have a double and two twin beds). Everything is freshly painted and in apple-pie order. During the summer, dinner is available with advance notice. There are a great variety of restaurants in nearby Westport. *Directions:* Westport is 100 kilometers northwest of Galway. The right-hand turn to Wilmaur is signposted 3 kilometers to the west of the town on the road to Croagh Patrick.

WILMAUR
Owner: Marie Printer
Rosbeg
Westport
Co Mayo
tel: (098) 25784
5 ensuite rooms
From £16.50 per person B&B
Open April to October
Credit cards: none
B&B

The owner's plans for Clonard House, begun in 1783, showed a grand three-story structure, but skirmishes with the British continually interrupted construction and depleted funds so he got no farther than the second floor, leaving the grand central staircase to curve into the ceiling. The massive front door opens to a smiling welcome from Kathleen Hayes who takes a great interest in her guests and pride in her home. I particularly admired her traditional, high-ceilinged sitting room with its peach-colored walls and traditional chairs covered in soft colors that coordinate with the draperies and carpet. Crisp white tablecloths top the little tables in the attractive dining room where guests enjoy traditional breakfasts and hearty dinners. The bedrooms are all attractively decorated and have TVs and ensuite showers or bathrooms. The five bedrooms that face the front of the house, while smaller in size, offer lovely views across farmland to the distant sea. Being just a short drive from Rosslare, Clonard House is ideal for your first or last nights in Ireland if you are arriving by ferry. Sightseeing attractions nearby include the Irish National Heritage Park, Wexford, and Johnstown Castle garden and agricultural museum. *Directions:* From Rosslare travel 13 kilometers towards Wexford, make a left at the first roundabout (N25), left at the second roundabout on to the R733, and immediately left to Clonard House.

CLONARD HOUSE **NEW**
Owners: Kathleen and John Hayes
Clonard Great
Wexford
Co Wexford
tel: (053) 47337 fax: (053) 43141
9 ensuite rooms
From £16 per person B&B
Open Easter to November
Credit cards: none
Farmhouse B&B

When Otto and Patricia built their home, they used a traditional Georgian design and gave it an old-fashioned feel with ceiling moldings, and traditional doors and decor. Friends suggested they open as a farm guesthouse, so taking the plunge, they added extra bathrooms and opened their doors. How fortunate they did, for now visitors to the Wicklow area can enjoy this welcoming home and garden that surrounds it. There are several restaurants in Wicklow, but if you make reservations in advance, Patricia, who loves to cook, prepares good, homey meals, with homemade soup, wiener schnitzel accompanied by farm-fresh vegetables, and plum pie being the order of the day for our meal. (Otto came to Ireland from East Germany, so Patricia enjoys serving a mixture of Irish and German dishes.) Portions are large enough to satisfy even the heartiest of eaters. The bedrooms are decorated in soft pastels, the orthopedic beds topped by soft woolen bedspreads. One guestroom has the advantage of a king-size bed and ensuite bathroom. Wicklow is a pleasant, small town 'round a harbor, just an hour's drive south of Dublin and the Dun Laoghaire ferry and north of the Rosslare ferry. The Wicklow Mountains, Powerscourt Gardens, Glendalough, and the Vale of Avoca are close at hand. *Directions:* As you enter Wicklow town turn right at the Grand Hotel, towards the top of the hill take the first right on Ashtown Lane, and Lissadell House is on your right .

LISSADELL HOUSE
Owners: Otto and Patricia Klaue
Ashtown Lane off Marlton Road
Wicklow
Co Wicklow
tel: (0404) 67458
4 rooms, 1 ensuite
From £16 per person B&B
Open March to November
Credit cards: none
Farmhouse B&B

Youghal (pronounced "you all" with an American southern drawl), a workaday fishing port, is beginning to flaunt its historic past: drab, gray buildings are being restored, empty shopfronts are coming to life, and, standing amongst them, Aherne's old-world pub exterior is decked out in shiny new paint. Aherne's pub, in the Fitzgibbon family since 1923, includes a seafood restaurant and bedrooms. There's an old-world, traditional atmosphere in the bars where you can enjoy a pint with the locals and an array of tempting barfood (food served 10:30 am to 10:30 pm). The restaurant specializes in locally caught seafood (lobster, prawns, turbot, salmon, monkfish, clams, and mussels) and the menu changes daily, depending on what is fresh and available. In the guests' sitting room, a cozy fire is flanked by comfortable sofas and a coffee table stacked with books on all things Irish. Three ground-floor bedrooms offer easy access, with one specially equipped for wheelchairs. I especially enjoyed the upstairs rooms which have little balconies facing the courtyard. All guestrooms have the most attractive decor, nice antique furniture, and large firm beds, each accompanied by an immaculate bathroom. Stop by the Visitors Centre and pick up a map which directs you on a walking tour of the walled port. *Directions:* Youghal is almost midway between Waterford and Cork on the N25. Aherne's is on the main street in town. Park in the brick courtyard.

AHERNE'S   **NEW**
Owners: Gaye, Kate, John, & David Fitzgibbon
163 North Main Street
Youghal
Co Cork
tel: (024) 92424 fax: (024) 93633
10 ensuite rooms
From £40 per person B&B
Open all year
Credit cards: EC, MC, VS
Restaurant with rooms

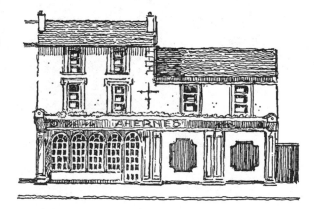

Blarney

206

Maps

- ● Places to Stay
- ○ Orientation
- ✈ Airport

Belfast

Dublin

Culdaff

Bushmills

Rathmullan

Coleraine

Ballymoney

Ramelton

Carnlough

Letterkenny ○

Raphoe

Stranolar

Bruckless

Donegal

Dunkineely

Dungannon

Rossnowlagh

LOUGH NEAGH

Belfast

Ballinamallard

Grange

Tempo

Eniskillen ○

Tamlaght

Sligo ○

Riverstown

Cavan

Ballymote

Carrick-on-Shannon

Map 1

Map 2

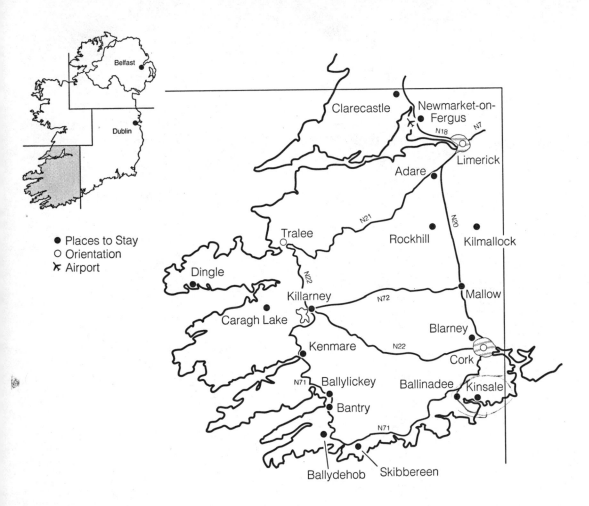

Places to Stay
Orientation
Airport

Belfast

Dublin

Clarecastle

Newmarket-on-Fergus

N18

N7

Limerick

Adare

N21

Tralee

Rockhill

Kilmallock

N20

Dingle

N22

Killarney

Caragh Lake

Kenmare

N72

Mallow

Blarney

N22

Cork

N71

Ballylickey

Ballinadee

Kinsale

Bantry

N71

Ballydehob

Skibbereen

Map 3

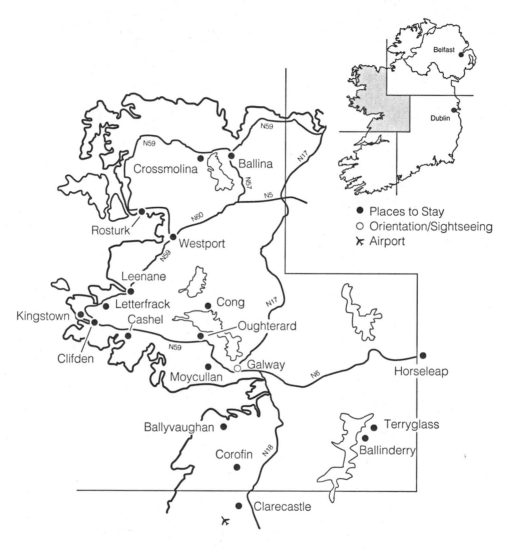

Map 4

Members of Hidden Ireland 1995

Listed alphabetically by house

Avondale House, Scribblestown, Dublin
Ballinkeele House, Ballymurn
Ballyvolane House, Castlelyons
Bantry House, Bantry
Blanchville House, Maddoxtown
Carnelly House, Clarecastle
Clohamon House, Bunclody
Delphi Lodge, Leenane
Enniscoe House, Crossmolina
Glendalough House, Caragh Lake
Gurthalougha House, Ballinderry
Lorum Old Rectory, Borris
Martinstown House, Curragh Camp
Mornington House, Mullingar
Moycullen House, Moycullen
Roundwood House, Mountrath
Temple House, Ballymote
Tempo Manor, Tempo
Thomond House, Newmarket-on-Fergus

Members of Irish Country Houses Association 1995

Listed alphabetically by house

Aherne's, Youghal
Ballymaloe House, Shanagarry
Blackheath House, Coleraine
Cashel House, Cashel
Coopershill, Riverstown
Currarevagh House, Oughterard
Doyle's Bar & Townhouse, Dingle
Enniscoe House, Crossmolina
Gregans Castle, Ballyvaughan
Longueville House, Mallow
Moyglare Manor, Maynooth
Marfield House, Gorey
Park Hotel, Kenmare
Rathmullan House, Rathmullan
Rosleague Manor, Letterfrack
St Ernan's House Hotel, Donegal
Tinakilly House, Rathnew

United States Hotel Representatives

BTH Hotels
800-221-1074
Ashford Castle, Cong
Dromoland Castle, Newmarket-on-Fergus
Waterford Castle, Waterford

Forte Hotels
800-225-5843
Shelbourne Hotel, Dublin

Prima Reservations
800-223-1588
Cahernane Hotel, Killarney
Dunraven Arms, Adare
Londonderry Arms, Carnlough
Rock Glen Hotel, Clifden
Sea View House Hotel, Ballylickey

Robert Reid Associates
800-223-6510
Aherne's, Youghal
Ballymaloe House, Shanagarry
Blackheath House, Coleraine
Cashel House, Cashel
Coopershill, Riverstown
Currarevagh House, Oughterard
Doyle's Bar & Townhouse, Dingle
Enniscoe House, Crossmolina
Gregans Castle, Ballyvaughan
Longueville House, Mallow
Moyglare Manor, Maynooth
Marfield House, Gorey
Park Hotel, Kenmare
Rathmullan House, Rathmullan
Rosleague Manor, Letterfrack
St Ernan's House Hotel, Donegal
Tinakilly House, Rathnew

Index

We love to hear from Karen Brown's readers

ACCOLADES: We'd love to hear which accommodations you have especially enjoyed—even the shortest of notes is greatly appreciated. It is reassuring to know that places we recommend meet with your approval.

COMPLAINTS: Please let us know when a place we recommend fails to live up to the standards you have come to expect from Karen Brown. Constructive criticism is greatly appreciated. We sometimes make a mistake, places change, or go downhill. Your letters influence us to re-evaluate a listing.

RECOMMENDATIONS: If you have a favorite hideaway that you would like to recommend, please write to us. Give us a feel for the place, if possible send us a brochure and photographs (which we regret we cannot return). Convince us that on our next research trip, your discovery deserves a visit. All accommodations included in our guides are ones we have seen and enjoyed. Many of our finest selections are those that readers have discovered—wonderful places we would never have found on our own.

Please send information to:

KAREN BROWN'S GUIDES
Post Office Box 70
San Mateo, California 94401, U.S.A.
Telephone (415) 342-9117   Fax (415) 342-9153

Be a Karen Brown's preferred reader

If you would like to be the first to know when new editions of Karen Brown's Guides go to press, and also to be included in any special promotions, simply send us your name and address. We encourage you to buy new editions and throw away the old ones. You'll be glad you did. Don't miss a wealth of wonderful new discoveries—or run the risk of staying in places that no longer meet our standards. We cover the miles searching for special places so that you don't have to spend your valuable vacation time doing so.

Name _____

Street _____

Town _____ State _____ Zip _____

Telephone: _____ Fax: _____

Please send information to:

KAREN BROWN'S GUIDES
Post Office Box 70
San Mateo, California 94401, U.S.A.
telephone (415) 342-9117   fax (415) 342-9153

Karen Brown's Country Inn Guides
The Most Reliable & Informative Series on Country Inns

Detailed itineraries guide you through the countryside. Every recommendation, from the most deluxe hotel to a simple B&B, is personally inspected, approved and chosen for its romantic ambiance and warmth of welcome. Our charming accommodations reflect every price range, from budget hideaways to the most luxurious palaces.

U.S.A. Order Form

Please ask in your local bookstore for KAREN BROWN'S GUIDES. If the books you want are unavailable, you may order directly from the publisher.

California Country Inns & Itineraries $14.95

English Country Bed & Breakfasts $15.95

English, Welsh & Scottish Country Hotels & Itineraries $14.95

French Country Bed & Breakfasts $15.95

French Country Inns & Itineraries $14.95

German Country Inns & Itineraries $14.95

Irish Country Inns & Itineraries $16.95

Italian Country Bed & Breakfasts $14.95

Italian Country Inns & Itineraries $16.95

Spanish Country Inns & Paradors $14.95

Swiss Country Inns & Itineraries $16.95

Name _____ Street _____

Town _____ State _____ Zip _____ tel. _____

Credit Card (MasterCard or Visa) _____ Exp: _____

Add $3.50 for the first book and .50 cents for each additional book for postage & packing. California residents add 8.25% sales tax. Order form only for shipments within the U.S.A. Indicate number of copies of each title; send form with check or credit card information to:

KAREN BROWN'S GUIDES
Post Office Box 70, San Mateo, California, 94401, U.S.A.
tel: (415) 342-9117   fax: (415) 342-9153

KAREN BROWN wrote her first travel guide in 1979. Her personalized travel series has grown to eleven titles and Karen and her small staff work diligently to keep all the guides updated. Karen, her husband, Rick, and their children Alexandra and Richard, live on the coast south of San Francisco at their own country inn, Seal Cove Inn, in Moss Beach.

JUNE BROWN hails from Sheffield, England, has an extensive background in travel, dating back to her school-girl days when she "youth hosteled" throughout Europe. June lives in San Mateo with her husband, Tony, and their children Simon and Clare.

BARBARA TAPP, the talented artist responsible for all the delightful illustrations in this guide, was raised in Australia where she studied interior design. Barbara works freelance as a pen and ink illustrator for real estate companies. She specializes in exteriors, interiors and gardens. Barbara lives in the San Francisco East Bay with her husband, Richard, and children Jonathan, Alexander and Georgia.

JANN POLLARD, the artist responsible for the cover painting, has studied art since childhood, and is well-known for her outstanding impressionistic-style water colors which she has exhibited in numerous juried shows, winning many awards. Jann travels frequently to Europe (using Karen Brown's guides) where she loves to paint. Jann lives in the Burlingame with her husband, Gene, and their two daughters.

SEAL COVE INN—LOCATED IN THE SAN FRANCISCO AREA

Karen Brown Herbert (best known as author of the Karen Brown's Guides) and her husband, Rick, have put seventeen years of experience into reality and opened their own superb hideaway, Seal Cove Inn. Spectacularly set amongst wild flowers and bordered by towering cypress trees, Seal Cove Inn looks out to the ocean over acres of county park: an oasis where you can enjoy secluded beaches, explore tide-pools, watch frolicking seals, and follow the tree-lined path that traces the windswept ocean bluffs. Country antiques, original-watercolors, flower-laden cradles, rich fabrics, and the gentle ticking of grandfather clocks create the perfect ambiance for a foggy day in front of a crackling log fire. Each bedroom is its own haven with a cozy sitting area before a wood-burning fireplace and doors opening onto a private balcony or patio with views to the distant ocean. Moss Beach is a 35-minute drive south of San Francisco, 6 miles north of the picturesque town of Half Moon Bay, and a few minutes from Princeton harbor with its colorful fishing boats and restaurants. Seal Cove Inn makes a perfect base for whale-watching, salmon-fishing excursions, day trips to San Francisco, exploring the coast, or best of all, just a romantic interlude by the sea, time to relax and be pampered. Karen and Rick look forward to the pleasure of welcoming you to their hideaway by the sea.

Seal Cove Inn, 221 Cypress Avenue, Moss Beach, California, 94038, U.S.A.
telephone: (415) 728-7325   fax: (415) 728-4116